# Legalines®

**Features Detailed Briefs of Every Major Case,
Plus Summaries of the Black Letter Law**

D1568149

## Titles Available

Administrative Law ................... Keyed to Breyer
Administrative Law ................... Keyed to Strauss
Administrative Law ................... Keyed to Schwartz
Antitrust ................................. Keyed to Areeda
Antitrust ................................. Keyed to Pitofsky
Business Associations .............. Keyed to Klein
Civil Procedure ........................ Keyed to Cound
Civil Procedure ........................ Keyed to Field
Civil Procedure ........................ Keyed to Hazard
Civil Procecure ........................ Keyed to Rosenberg
Civil Procedure ........................ Keyed to Yeazell
Conflict of Laws ....................... Keyed to Currie
Conflict of Laws ....................... Keyed to Hay
Constitutional Law .................... Keyed to Brest
Constitutional Law .................... Keyed to Choper
Constitutional Law .................... Keyed to Cohen
Constitutional Law .................... Keyed to Rotunda
Constitutional Law .................... Keyed to Stone
Constitutional Law .................... Keyed to Sullivan
Contracts ................................ Keyed to Calamari
Contracts ................................ Keyed to Dawson
Contracts ................................ Keyed to Farnsworth
Contracts ................................ Keyed to Fuller
Contracts ................................ Keyed to Kessler
Contracts ................................ Keyed to Murphy
Corporations ........................... Keyed to Choper
Corporations ........................... Keyed to Eisenberg
Corporations ........................... Keyed to Hamilton
Corporations ........................... Keyed to Vagts
Criminal Law ........................... Keyed to Johnson

Criminal Law ........................... Keyed to Kadish
Criminal Law ........................... Keyed to LaFave
Criminal Procedure .................. Keyed to Kamisar
Decedents' Estates & Trusts ..... Keyed to Dobris
Domestic Relations .................. Keyed to Wadlington
Evidence ................................. Keyed to Waltz
Evidence ................................. Keyed to Weinstein
Evidence ................................. Keyed to Wellborn
Family Law .............................. Keyed to Areen
Federal Courts ......................... Keyed to Wright
Income Tax .............................. Keyed to Freeland
Income Tax .............................. Keyed to Klein
Labor Law ............................... Keyed to Cox
Labor Law ............................... Keyed to St. Antoine
Property .................................. Keyed to Casner
Property .................................. Keyed to Cribbet
Property .................................. Keyed to Dukeminier
Property .................................. Keyed to Nelson
Property .................................. Keyed to Rabin
Remedies ................................ Keyed to Re
Remedies ................................ Keyed to Rendelman
Sales & Secured Transactions .. Keyed to Speidel
Securities Regulation ................ Keyed to Coffee
Torts ...................................... Keyed to Dobbs
Torts ...................................... Keyed to Epstein
Torts ...................................... Keyed to Franklin
Torts ...................................... Keyed to Henderson
Torts ...................................... Keyed to Keeton
Torts ...................................... Keyed to Prosser
Wills, Trusts & Estates .............. Keyed to Dukeminier

*All Titles Available at Your Law School Bookstore*

**THOMSON**

**WEST**

111 W. Jackson Boulevard, 7th Floor
Chicago, IL 60604

# Legalines

*Editorial Advisors:*
**Gloria A. Aluise**
Attorney at Law
**Jonathan Neville**
Attorney at Law
**Robert A. Wyler**
Attorney at Law

*Authors:*
**Gloria A. Aluise**
Attorney at Law
**Daniel O. Bernstine**
Attorney at Law
**Roy L. Brooks**
Professor of Law
**Scott M. Burbank**
C.P.A.
**Charles N. Carnes**
Professor of Law
**Paul S. Dempsey**
Professor of Law
**Jerome A. Hoffman**
Professor of Law
**Mark R. Lee**
Professor of Law
**Jonathan Neville**
Attorney at Law
**Laurence C. Nolan**
Professor of Law
**Arpiar Saunders**
Attorney at Law
**Robert A. Wyler**
Attorney at Law

# EVIDENCE

## Adaptable to Fifth Edition* of Mueller Casebook

By Jonathan Neville
Attorney at Law

*If your casebook is a newer edition, go to www.gilbertlaw.com to see if a supplement is available for this title.

THOMSON

WEST

EDITORIAL OFFICES: 111 W. Jackson Blvd., 7th Floor, Chicago, IL 60604
REGIONAL OFFICES: Chicago, Dallas, Los Angeles, New York, Washington, D.C.

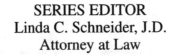

SERIES EDITOR
Linda C. Schneider, J.D.
Attorney at Law

PRODUCTION MANAGER
Elizabeth G. Duke

FIRST PRINTING—2007

# SHORT SUMMARY OF CONTENTS

# TABLE OF CONTENTS AND SHORT REVIEW OUTLINE

# I. EVIDENCE LAW AND THE SYSTEM

## A. DEVELOPMENT OF RULES OF EVIDENCE

1. **Basic Issue.** The basic issue in most evidence problems is whether the evidence is admissible. In trials, factual determinations are made by the jury (or the judge in a non-jury trial) based on the consideration only of admissible evidence. Principles of law are then applied to the facts to produce a judgment. Rules of evidence govern what evidence can actually be considered by the trier of fact in making its determination.

2. **Development of Evidence Rules.** Historically, the rules of evidence were judge-made products of the common law. Attempts at codification began in 1942; although several states adopted evidence codes, the California Evidence Code was the most notable. The United States Supreme Court developed the Federal Rules of Evidence ("Federal Rules"), which were adopted by Congress and became effective July 1, 1975. Many of the states have now adopted codes patterned after the Federal Rules. Despite this codification, study of the case law is essential to interpret the rules and to understand the policies underlying the rules.

## B. EVIDENCE RULES AND MAKING A RECORD

1. **Description of the Record.** The possibility of appeal makes it critical that all matters involved in a trial be recorded. Appellate courts can only act upon an official record of the trial. The record includes all the litigation paperwork, including the pleadings (complaint, answer, etc.), written motions and briefs, and proposed jury instructions. It also contains the verbatim transcript of what happened at the trial, including arguments, testimony, instructions, and any other spoken words. Typically, the transcript makes up the majority of the record. Finally, the exhibits offered into evidence are included in the record. The record needs to be accurate and comprehensive, because appellate courts limit review to what is contained in the record.

2. **Dual Objectives of the Trial Lawyer.** Naturally, a trial lawyer concentrates on doing everything possible to prevail at trial. However, even the simplest trial presents numerous opportunities for error that might justify an appeal. The trial lawyer must conduct the trial with an eye toward a possible appeal. Thus, constructing an effective record of trial is a second objective of the trial lawyer. Much of what takes place during a trial is done solely to make a favorable record. A large number of appeals are based on evidentiary rulings, so the effective trial counsel must be able to use the rules of evidence in constructing a favorable record of trial. For an appellate court to

review such appeals, there must have been, at the trial stage, a specific, timely objection, based on a valid ground, and the trial court's error must have been prejudicial.

3.   **Evidence Procedure.** Admissibility questions arise when one party offers evidence and the other party objects. If the judge sustains the objection, the evidence is not admitted, meaning that the fact finder may not consider the evidence. If the objection is overruled, the evidence is admitted and considered by the fact finder. Even when admitted, however, the weight and credibility of the evidence is left to the fact finder. Admission of evidence does not necessarily mean that the evidence is true and will be believed. Evidence is offered in four basic ways:

a.   **Direct examination of witnesses.** Testimony of witnesses is obtained through the witnesses' response to questions of counsel. Counsel's questioning of his or her own witness is called direct examination. The questions must be fairly specific so that opposing counsel has an idea of what the response will be and can object before the witness answers if the answer would be inadmissible. There are certain restrictions on the kinds of questions that can be asked on direct examination. The rules differ as to expert witnesses, however; expert witnesses are discussed in the last chapter of this outline.

1)   **Leading questions.** On direct examination, counsel may not ask leading questions, or questions that suggest their own answers. For example, counsel could not normally ask, "You saw the defendant driving a blue car, didn't you?" or "Did you or did you not see the defendant driving a blue car?" However, it is permissible to direct the witness's attention to a particular date and then ask whether anything unusual occurred, as long as the answer is not suggested in the question. Despite the general rule, leading questions may be asked on direct examination in the following situations:

a)   **Preliminary matters.** Preliminary questions can be used to establish the basic background of the witness, such as employment, length of time in the community, etc., as long as this information is not critical to the case.

b)   **Undisputed matters.** To connect with earlier testimony, a leading question may be used as long as the matter is undisputed; *e.g.,* "You testified earlier that you were at the scene, didn't you?"

c)   **Hostile witness.** If the witness is hostile or adverse, there is little likelihood that she would accept a false "lead," so leading questions may be used. [Fed. R. Evid. 611(c)] Along the same lines, if the witness gives a "surprise" answer, a leading question may be permitted.

    **d)**    **Difficulty in testifying.** If the witness has difficulty testifying, such as a witness who does not speak English well, or a child, leading questions may be used as necessary.

    **e)**    **Exhausted recollection.** If the witness indicates she has more knowledge, but has exhausted her recollection of that knowledge, a leading question may be used (with permission of the judge) to refresh recollection.

**2)**    **Compound questions.** Examination of witnesses is intended to produce succinct answers to specific questions. It is improper (and ineffective) to ask several questions as part of one question. This confuses the witness and the court and makes it difficult for opposing counsel to properly object.

**3)**    **Assuming unproved facts.** Counsel cannot testify by asking a witness questions that assume facts not yet proved.

**b.**    **Cross-examination of witnesses.** Cross-examination is less restricted than direct examination, although the questions must not range too far beyond the scope of the direct examination. Leading questions are permitted. Questions affecting the witness's credibility, including existence of bias, interest in the litigation, or inaccurate perception, are appropriate, as well as questions revealing inconsistent prior statements or convictions for crimes involving falsehood.

**c.**    **Tangible evidence.** Tangible evidence is evidence that can be held and seen, as opposed to the oral testimony of witnesses. There are three types of tangible evidence:

**1)**    **Real evidence.** Real evidence is the actual thing it purports to be, *e.g.,* the murder weapon, the defective part, etc. Such evidence—exhibits—must be marked either before or at the time of introduction. Exhibits are first marked for identification; if admitted, the "for identification" marking is removed or lined out. Exhibits are normally offered through a witness who can identify them. The questioning of the identifying witness is called "laying a foundation" for the evidence. In other words, counsel cannot merely stand up and say, "I offer the murder weapon as evidence" without a witness's identification and description of the item.

**2)**    **Demonstrative evidence.** Demonstrative evidence is used to explain or illustrate a point. Typical examples are maps, diagrams, models, etc. Demonstrative evidence may be prepared by the attorneys, although assurances as to accuracy must be included as part of the foundation.

> 3) **Writings.** A writing must be authenticated before it can be considered by the fact finder. This means that the court must be satisfied as to the genuineness of the writing before it will be admitted. There are various ways this can be done. Articles IX and X of the Federal Rules govern this area.

> d.  **Judicial notice.** Judges are allowed to take notice, without formal proof, of certain matters that are either subject to common knowledge among reasonably informed persons in the jurisdiction or capable of accurate and ready determination by resort to sources whose accuracy cannot reasonably be disputed. The judge may require some information; *e.g.,* a calendar may be used if counsel requests judicial notice of the day of the week a particular date fell on.

4.  **Objections.** As mentioned previously, counsel must object to any evidence he or she does not want the court to admit. The objection must be made after the evidence is offered and before it is admitted, although it is possible to make preliminary motions to exclude evidence expected to be offered. Failure to object in a timely manner may constitute waiver of the objection. However, if the inadmissibility of the evidence becomes apparent only after it has been received, such as when on cross-examination the witness admits that her knowledge was based on hearsay rather than direct observation, counsel can move to have the inadmissible testimony removed from the consideration of the fact finder. Normally the counsel objecting must specify the grounds for the objection; objecting on grounds of irrelevancy will not cover all possible grounds. If an objection is overruled because the ground given does not apply, most courts hold that there is no reversible error even if there was another ground that would properly have required rejection of the evidence.

5.  **Offer of Proof.** When the proponent of evidence is unable to overcome an objection, he can make an offer of proof to show the trial court (but more importantly the appellate court) what the evidence would have been had it been admitted. This offer is of course not made known to the fact finder for consideration. The offer of proof enables an appellate court to determine whether, if the court erred in excluding the evidence, such error was prejudicial. A judgment will not be reversed if the errors committed were harmless.

6.  **Appellate Review.** The various rules of evidence will be discussed throughout the remainder of this outline. In applying the rules, however, the following requirements for reversal on appeal for the improper receipt of evidence should always be kept in mind:

a.  A specific objection;

b. Timely made;

c. Based on a valid ground; and

d. Prejudice resulting from the error in overruling the objection.

# II. RELEVANCE

## A. EVIDENCE RELEVANT TO ISSUES IN THE CASE

1. **Introduction.** To be admissible, all evidence that is offered, of whatever kind *(e.g.*, testimony of witnesses, real evidence, etc.), must be relevant. Furthermore, all relevant evidence is admissible unless there is a legal reason to exclude it. The determination of relevancy depends on two concepts that were once clearly distinguished under common law but that now, under Federal Rule 401, are part of a single test: "materiality" and "probativeness." The Rule states: "'Relevant evidence' means evidence having any tendency to make the existence of any fact that is of consequence to the determination of the action more probable or less probable than it would be without the evidence."

2. **Materiality.** To be admissible, evidence must be material, *i.e.,* offered to prove a properly provable issue in the case. In other words, the evidence must prove something that relates to an issue in the case.

    a. **Issues presented at trial.** The object of a trial is to elicit the truth about issues presented to reach judgment or decision. The issues are framed by the pleadings, the applicable legal principles, and sometimes by pre-trial orders.

    b. **Nonmaterial evidence.** Matters not included within this framework are not issues in the case; *e.g.,* when a plaintiff sues a defendant on a written contract, and the only defense pleaded by the defendant is a denial that he executed the contract, evidence offered by him as to a release of liability from the contract would be immaterial and thus irrelevant.

3. **Nature of Legal Evidence**. In *Evidence and Inference in the Law,* Hart and McNaughton (1958), the authors point out that legal evidence differs significantly from scientific evidence. Although some scientific evidence may be used in courts, the objective of litigation is to solve disputes, not to discover ultimate truths. Evidence in the legal context is necessarily limited to whatever the parties decide to present. The time constraints inherent in the litigation process do not permit repetitive experimentation and extensive research. The law compromises certainty in favor of dispute resolution. Hence the use of standards of proof: "beyond a reasonable doubt" and "preponderance of the evidence." The law also relies on lay juries to make factual conclusions instead of trained experts. The rules of evidence are intended to assist in dispute resolution even when they may result in exclusion of "proof" of what really happened.

4. **Determining Issues of the Case.** In *Relevancy, Probability and the Law*, James, 29 Cal. L. Rev. 689 (1941), James states that exclusion of evidence as irrelevant would be for the following reasons: it is not probative of the proposition at which it is directed, or the proposition in question is not provable in the case. In one case involving a breach of warranty for paint, the trial court excluded evidence of a defective drum of paint purchased six months prior to the drum involved in the case. The appellate court reversed, holding that a person might hesitate before using the second drum based on the experience with the first drum. What this court actually did was apply a novel rule of substantive law through the instrumentality of a rule of evidence.

## B. RELEVANCE AND INFERENCE

1. **Probative Value.** Besides being material, relevant evidence must be probative. This means that it must logically tend to prove the proposition for which it is offered. The evidence need not be determinative; it need only make the fact to which it is directed more likely than it would be without that evidence. If the evidence would support an inference of the ultimate fact to be proven, for example, it is probably sufficiently probative to be relevant.

2. **Inferences.** It is not uncommon to rely on inferences to prove a case. The following areas are fruitful ground for inferences: ability and opportunity, motive, design, plan or scheme, intent, and mental and physical condition.

3. **Relevance for Jury's Understanding--**

## Old Chief v. United States (I), 519 U.S. 172 (1997).

**Facts.** Old Chief (D) was charged with violating a federal statute that prohibits possession of a firearm by anyone who has a prior felony conviction. He offered to stipulate that he had a prior conviction. The government refused to accept the stipulation, claiming a right to present evidence of the prior conviction, including the name and nature of the prior offense.

**Issue.** Is the name of a crime of which a defendant was previously convicted relevant to the prior-conviction element of a case?

**Held.** Yes. However, judgment reversed due to unfair prejudice. (*See* Old Chief (II), *infra*.)

♦ Under Federal Rule 401, the name of the prior offense was relevant because it made D's status under the statute more probable than it would have been without the evidence.

♦ D's offer of a stipulation did not affect the evidentiary relevance of the government's evidence. Even if the stipulation satisfied that element of the offense, the government may need to offer the detailed evidence to convince the jury that a guilty verdict would be morally reasonable and to satisfy the jury's expectations regarding what proper proof should be.

---

# C. PROBATIVE VALUE VS. PREJUDICIAL EFFECT

1. **Introduction.** There are several specific exclusionary rules which will be discussed, *infra*. However, Federal Rule 403 gives a trial judge broad discretion to exclude relevant evidence when its probative value is substantially outweighed by the danger of unfair prejudice, confusion of the issues, or misleading the jury, or by considerations of undue delay, waste of time, or needless presentation of cumulative evidence. The appellate courts will reverse these determinations only if the judge abuses her discretion.

2. **Exclusion of Prejudicial Relevant Evidence**

---

## State v. Chapple, 660 P.2d 1208 (Ariz. 1983)

---

**Facts.** Varnes was found dead of a gunshot wound to the head, apparently over a drug-money dispute. An individual known as "Dee" told Buck, who was involved in the drug transaction, that he had shot Varnes in the head. Chapple (D) was identified as "Dee" by Buck and another individual involved in the transaction. D defended on the ground that he was in another state at the time of the conviction. The trial court admitted graphic photographs of Varnes's charred body and his skull. D was convicted and appeals.

**Issue.** Are relevant, but inflammatory, photographs admissible where their probative value is low?

**Held.** No. Judgment reversed.

♦ Because the photographs depict the atrociousness of the act, they help establish first degree murder. Furthermore, they are useful to show that Varnes was shot in the head, which links the shooting to Dee. Therefore, the photographs are relevant to issues in the case.

♦ The photographs have little probative value because neither the fact that Varnes was killed nor the state of his body after he was killed are in controversy. Furthermore, they are not relevant to Buck's statement that Dee admitted that he had shot Varnes in the head. D claimed only that he was not Dee.

- Because this case turned on identification, the photographs only presented cumulative evidence on uncontroverted issues. The photographs served only to inflame the jurors and their admission was in error.

---

### 3. Exclusion of Relevant Evidence--

## Old Chief v. United States (II), 519 U.S. 172 (1997).

**Facts.** Old Chief (D) was arrested after a fight in which he used a firearm. He was charged with assault with a dangerous weapon and using a firearm. Because he had previously been convicted of assault causing serious bodily injury, a felony punishable by imprisonment for more that one year, D was also charged with violating 18 U.S.C. section 922(g)(1), which prohibits possession of a firearm by anyone with a prior felony conviction. Before his trial, D moved for an order preventing the prosecution from mentioning his prior criminal conviction except to state that he had been convicted of a crime punishable by imprisonment exceeding one year. He also offered to stipulate to the fact of that conviction. The prosecution refused to join the stipulation, and the district court allowed the prosecution's evidence about the name of D's prior conviction. The Ninth Circuit affirmed. The Supreme Court granted certiorari.

**Issue.** If a defendant offers to stipulate to the fact of a prior felony conviction to prove the element of prior conviction needed by the prosecution, may the prosecution still admit the full record of the prior conviction when the name or nature of the prior offense raises the risk of a verdict tainted by improper considerations?

**Held.** No. Judgment reversed.

- The name of D's prior offense was clearly relevant in the sense that it made his status under section 922(g)(1) more probable than it would have been without the evidence. This relevance is unaffected by the availability of alternative proofs of the element to which it goes. The inadmissibility of relevant evidence must rest not on the ground that alternative evidence has made it irrelevant, but on its character as unfairly prejudicial or cumulative.

- Rule 403 allows exclusion of relevant evidence when its "probative value is substantially outweighed by the danger of unfair prejudice, confusion of the issues, or misleading the jury, or by considerations of undue delay, waste of time, or needless presentation of cumulative evidence." In the criminal context, unfair prejudice means an undue tendency to suggest decision on an improper basis.

- D asserts that the disclosure of the name of his prior offense allowed the jury to generalize his prior bad act into bad character that increased the probability of his doing the later bad act he was being tried for. The common law tradition disallows the prosecution from resorting to any kind of evidence of a defendant's evil character to establish a probability of his guilt. Thus, Rule 404(b) specifically prohibits the admission of evidence of other crimes to prove the character of a person in order to show action in conformity therewith.

- ◆ In determining the admissibility of relevant evidence, the court should consider a party's concession of the point under Rule 401. Under Rule 403, the court may consider the availability of alternative means of proof when deciding whether to exclude on grounds of unfair prejudice. Under Rule 404, the court must consider the dual nature of legitimate evidence of an element and illegitimate evidence of character.

- ◆ Under section 922(g)(1), evidence of the name or nature of the prior offense generally carries a risk of unfair prejudice to the defendant. In this case, D's preferred admission would have been conclusive evidence of the element.

- ◆ The prosecution notes that it has the right to prove its case by evidence of its own choice. While this is an important rule regarding the facts of a case, it does not apply to the issue of a defendant's legal status that depends on a judgment rendered wholly independently of the concrete events of later criminal behavior charged against him. The only issue was whether D fell within section 922(g)(1), and the only thing the jury needed to know was that the conviction admitted by D fell within that statute. Therefore, it was an abuse of discretion to admit the record of the conviction when an admission was available.

**Dissent** (O'Connor, Thomas, JJ., Scalia, C.J.). Distinctions among felonies are important, and a jury is likely to be puzzled by missing information regarding a prior felony conviction.

---

## D. PROBABILISTIC EVIDENCE

1. **Introduction.** When a certain event cannot be proved by direct evidence, the parties may resort to proof based on probabilities. Such evidence is not favored, even though the standard of proof in a civil case may be "more likely than not"; the courts require more certainty than a mere statistical likelihood. However, if in a given case the probability evidence is such that it approaches certainty, the courts will admit the evidence.

2. **Rejected in Criminal Case--**

**People v. Collins**, 438 P.2d 33 (Cal. 1968).

**Facts.** Collins (D), who was black with a beard and mustache, and his wife, who was Caucasian with a blond ponytail, were convicted of second degree robbery. The prosecution had difficulty establishing the identities of the perpetrators of the crime, and in an attempt to bolster the identifications, the prosecution called a mathematician as a witness to introduce probability theory. The prosecution, by use of estimated probabilities, theorized that only one couple in 12 million possessed the characteristics of D and his wife; therefore, there was only one chance in 12 million that D was innocent. The prosecution's theory was based on the "product rule" of probabilities; *i.e.*, the probability of the joint occurrence of mutually independent events is equal to the product of the individual probabilities that each of the events will occur. The estimated probabilities were as follows:

(i)   Partly yellow car .1,

(ii)  Man with mustache .25,

(iii) Woman with ponytail .1,

(iv)  Blond woman .33,

(v)   Bearded black man .1,

(vi)  Interracial couple in car .001.

No evidence was introduced as to the reasonableness of the above estimates. D appeals.

**Issue.** May a criminal conviction rely on probability theory, which does not exclude all possible perpetrators but the defendant?

**Held.** No. Judgment reversed.

♦   The probability statistics injected two fundamental prejudicial errors into the case:

(i)   The testimony lacked an adequate foundation in evidence and in statistical theory. The prosecution produced no evidence from which it could be inferred that the estimates used were correct. Mathematical odds are not admissible as evidence to identify a defendant when the odds are based on estimates the validity of which have not been demonstrated. Furthermore, there was inadequate proof of the statistical independence of the six factors.

(ii)  The testimony distracted the jury from its proper and requisite function of weighing the evidence on the issue of guilt. Without an adequate evidentiary foundation and without proof of statistical independence, the testimony could only lead to wild conjecture without demonstrated relevancy to the issues presented. The introduction of the probability theory distracted the jury from weighing the credibility of the prosecution witnesses and assessing the guilt of the defendants upon the evidence presented.

◆ The probability computed by the prosecution could represent, at best, the likelihood that a random couple would share the characteristics described by the People's witnesses—not necessarily the characteristics of the actually guilty couple. The evidence did not help the jury decide which, if any, of the admittedly few such couples was guilty of committing the robbery.

---

# III. HEARSAY

## A. BASIC PRINCIPLES

1. **Significance.** Otherwise relevant evidence may be excluded upon timely objection if it is hearsay. It is critical for a lawyer to understand the hearsay rules both to know what evidence he or she may use in trial, and to know what evidence the opponent offers may be excluded. Rule 802 provides that:

    > Hearsay is not admissible except as provided by these rules or by other rules prescribed by the Supreme Court pursuant to statutory authority or by Act of Congress.

2. **Definitions.** The basic definitions of hearsay are contained in Rule 801. Although the definitions may appear clear, application to specific cases can be difficult.

    a.  Rule 801(a) provides: A "statement" is

        (1) An oral or written assertion or

        (2) Nonverbal conduct of a person, if it is intended by the person as an assertion.

    b.  Rule 801(b) provides: A "declarant" is a person who makes a statement.

    c.  Rule 801(c) provides: "Hearsay" is a statement, other than one made by the declarant while testifying at the trial or hearing, offered in evidence to prove the truth of the matter asserted.

## B. DETERMINING WHAT IS A STATEMENT

1. **Assertive Conduct.** According to the orthodox definition, an "assertion" includes words, spoken or written, as well as conduct intended to communicate an assertion, so-called "assertive conduct." Rule 801(a)(2) takes this approach.

2. **Nonassertive Conduct.** One approach extends the notion of "assertion" to include conduct that is not intended to communicate an assertion, so-called "nonassertive conduct."

    a.  **Letters--**

**Wright v. Doe D. Tatham**, 112 Eng. Rep. 488 (Ex. Ch. 1837).

**Facts.** In a will contest, one claimant asserted that Marsden, a testator, was insane. Letters from third parties to Marsden written 22 years prior to the date of the will were offered to show that the writers thought Marsden was sane. The letters were not admitted.

**Issue.** Are letters hearsay when the contents are offered to prove that the writers thought the recipient was sane?

**Held.** Yes. Judgment affirmed.

- Evidence must be given under oath in court. The writers were not present in court and were not sworn.

- The issue was not Marsden's reputation, but whether Marsden was in fact sane. These letters were not originally intended to show that Marsden was sane, but because the writers treated him as mentally competent, they were offered to prove he was sane. This nonassertive conduct is hearsay, not within any exception.

---

### b. Lack of complaints by other customers--

## Cain v. George, 411 F.2d 572 (5th Cir. 1969).

**Facts.** The Cains (Ps) sued the Georges (Ds), the owners of a motel, claiming that Ps' son died of carbon monoxide poisoning due to Ds' negligence. A chair next to the heater in the guest room had burned. Ps claimed that the heater was defective and produced the carbon monoxide. Ds claimed the burning chair produced the gas. At trial, the court allowed Ds to testify about the number of guests who had previously occupied the room without complaint. The jury found that the death was an unavoidable accident, not proximately caused by anyone's negligence. Ps appeal, claiming that Ds' testimony regarding the lack of complaints was inadmissible hearsay.

**Issue.** Does a defendant's testimony about a lack of complaints by other customers constitute hearsay?

**Held.** No. Judgment affirmed.

- Ds' testimony was relevant on the issue of the source of the carbon monoxide. It related Ds' knowledge regarding whether anyone had ever been harmed by the heater before this incident.

- The testimony was not hearsay because it derived its value solely from the credibility of the witnesses themselves. It was not dependent upon the veracity or competency of other persons. Ds' testimony was the best available evidence to support their position that the heater was not the source of the carbon monoxide and how the heater had operated in the past.

---

3.    **Indirect Hearsay.**

    a.    **Introduction.** A witness who is asked her birth date would likely be allowed to reply, although the witness could not have firsthand knowledge of that date. Technically, such an answer would be hearsay, but unless the date is a contested matter in the case, no one is likely to object. An objection for lack of personal knowledge under Rule 602 might be more appropriate anyway. A greater problem arises when a witness attempts to testify about his own actual statements made in response to an out-of-court declarant's questions. In this case, the witness's testimony would not be technically hearsay, but it would have the effect of introducing hearsay indirectly.

    b.    **One side of telephone conversation--**

---

## United States v. Check, 582 F.2d 668 (2nd Cir. 1978).

**Facts.** Check (D) was a New York City policeman who was charged with possessing cocaine with intent to distribute. Spinelli, a detective, had been assigned to investigate D and went undercover as a prospective drug buyer. At trial, Spinelli testified that his informant, Cali, had engaged in conversations with D, and then Cali came to Spinelli to discuss those conversations. Cali did not testify at trial. However, the prosecutor had Spinelli testify about what he, Spinelli, said to Cali in those conversations. Spinelli's testimony included facts that Spinelli learned from Cali. D was convicted. D appeals, claiming Spinelli's testimony was hearsay.

**Issue.** May a party avoid a hearsay objection by having the witness testify as to what the witness himself said in an out-of-court conversation, where such testimony necessarily includes information provided by the other party to the conversation?

**Held.** No. Judgment reversed.

♦    The judge noted that Spinelli's testimony was weaving both sides of the conversation together. The prosecution itself made inferences about D's activity from Spinelli's testimony. The prosecution also offered, through Spinelli's testimony, the out-of-court statements made by Cali to prove the truth of the matters asserted therein.

♦    This testimony was clearly hearsay, and the artifice of having Spinelli supposedly restrict his testimony to his half of his conversations with Cali does not change the nature of the testimony. There is no hearsay exception for testimony regarding one-half of a conversation.

- ♦ The court should have granted D's motion to strike all of Spinelli's testimony regarding his conversations with Cali.

---

## C.  DISTINGUISHING HEARSAY AND NONHEARSAY

1. **Nonhearsay Statements.** A statement is hearsay under Rule 801 when it is "offered to prove the truth of the matter asserted." Courts have held that a statement is not hearsay if it is offered for other purposes, including the following:

   a.   Impeachment;

   b.   Verbal acts;

   c.   Effect on the hearer or reader;

   d.   Verbal objects; and

   e.   Circumstantial evidence of state of mind, memory, or belief.

2. **Statements Combined with Acts--**

---

**United States v. Singer**, 687 F.2d 1135, modified, 710 F.2d 431 (8th Cir. 1983).

---

**Facts.** Singer (D) and others, including Sazenski and Izquierdo, the latter who apparently used the alias "Almaden," were prosecuted for drug offenses. At trial, the court admitted into evidence an envelope addressed to Sazenski and Almaden at Sazenski's residence in Minnetonka, Minnesota. The envelope contained a notice to terminate their tenancy, and the evidence was introduced to show that Almaden lived with Sazenski. The envelope was found at the residence. Sazenski objected on hearsay grounds. Ds were convicted. Sazenski appeals.

**Issue.** May an envelope addressed to a defendant be used as evidence that the defendant did, in fact, reside at the address?

**Held.** Yes. Judgment affirmed.

- ♦ Hearsay is defined in terms of a "statement," so evidence of conduct not intended as an assertion is excluded from the hearsay rule. Nonverbal conduct may be offered as evidence that the actor believed in the existence of the condition sought to be proved, supporting an inference that the condition did exist.

♦ There is some guarantee that an inference drawn from out-of-court behavior is trustworthy because people base their actions on the correctness of their beliefs. The letter in this case could not properly be used to assert the implied truth of its written contents, but it can be used to imply from the landlord's behavior of sending the letter that Almaden lived at that address.

**Comments.**

♦ The conviction was reversed on appeal, but the court reaffirmed the portion of this opinion dealing with the hearsay rule.

♦ Note that it was the act of mailing the notice that made a difference. If an agent had asked an out-of-court declarant where Almaden lived, the answer would have been hearsay. But if the agent had discovered where Almaden lived by following someone who was delivering a package to Almaden, he could testify about what he saw.

---

3. **Statements to Prove Assumptions--**

**United States v. Pacelli**, 491 F.2d 1108 (2nd Cir. 1974), *cert. denied*, 419 U.S. 826 (1974).

**Facts.** Pacelli (D) had been indicted for drug offenses based in part on testimony given by Parks. Parks was found dead. She had been stabbed and her body had been burned. D was charged with conspiracy to interfere with Parks's constitutional rights in connection with Parks's murder. At trial, the court allowed Lipsky to testify about the conduct and statements of D's wife, uncle, and friends in February 1972. The testimony was intended to show that persons other than Lipsky believed D had murdered Parks. None of these statements suggested that any of these out-of-court declarants observed D commit the crimes. D was convicted. D appeals.

**Issue.** May testimony about statements made by out-of-court declarants be admitted to support an inference that the declarants believed certain facts?

**Held.** No. Judgment reversed.

♦ The conspiracy to violate Parks's civil rights terminated with Parks's death, so Lipsky's testimony was not admissible as declarations of co-conspirators made in the course of a conspiracy, or as evidence of illegal acts. The prosecution used this testimony to show the jury that people other than Lipsky believed D was guilty of the murder.

- The extra-judicial statements that Lipsky testified about implied knowledge and belief on the part of the third-person declarants, but the declarants were not available for cross-examination as to the source of their knowledge. This evidence violates the central purpose of the hearsay rule. Despite the prosecution's assertion that D alone could have provided the information these declarants relied on, cross-examination might have revealed several alternative sources.

- It is irrelevant that these extra-judicial statements may not have been intended by those who made them to communicate their belief that D murdered Parks. The danger of insincerity might be reduced where the assertions are implied instead of express, but there is an added danger of misinterpretation of the declarants' belief where they cannot be cross-examined. These statements have little indicia of reliability.

**Dissent** (Moore, J.). The statements Lipsky testified about were made after the newspapers had already reported on Parks's death, including the burning of her body. Lipsky did not testify that any of the declarants said D admitted killing Parks, and none expressed such an opinion. While this testimony should not have been admitted, its significance is minimal compared with Lipsky's eye-witness testimony, and there is no reversible error.

---

### 4. Statements as Circumstantial Evidence of State of Mind--

**Betts v. Betts**, 473 P.2d 403 (Wash. App. 1970).

**Facts.** Michael Betts (P) sued his former wife Rita Betts (D) for custody of their five-year-old daughter Tracey Lynn. D's boyfriend had been tried and acquitted for the murder of P's two-year-old son. At the trial, Tracey Lynn's foster mother testified that when she told the girl that D had married the boyfriend, the girl started crying and said "He killed my brother and he'll kill my mommie too." The court awarded custody to P. D appeals, claiming the foster mother's testimony should not have been admitted.

**Issue.** May statements by an out-of-court declarant be admitted to show the mental state of the declarant?

**Held.** Yes. Judgment affirmed.

- The testimony about the child's statements was not admitted to prove the truth of her assertions, but to show her mental state. The fact that she made these statements would tend to create a strained relationship between her and her stepfather and mother.

- Statements that circumstantially indicate a present state of mind regardless of their truth are nonhearsay statements. Statements that indicate a state of mind because of their truth are hearsay. The two types of statements can be distinguished by whether the statement shows the mental state regardless of the truth of the statement.

♦ In this case, Tracey Lynn's statements were nonhearsay because they circumstantially indicated a state of mind regardless of their truth. As such, these statements do not need to come within an exception to the hearsay rule. The mental state of the child was an important element in the decision to award custody.

**Comment.** If Tracey Lynn's statements had been deemed hearsay, they might have come within the exception for "excited utterances" or the exception for statements describing the declarant's state of mind. Then the court would have had to consider whether, as a five-year-old child, she would have been a competent witness.

---

# IV. HEARSAY EXCEPTIONS

## A. EXCEPTIONS WHEN DECLARANT TESTIFIES

1. **Introduction.** The definitions section of Rule 801 expressly excludes certain types of statements from the definition of hearsay. These statements would otherwise fall within the definition of hearsay. As defined in Rule 801(d), these statements fall into two categories: (i) prior statements by a witness, and (ii) admissions by a party-opponent.

   a. **Basic rule.** Rule 801(d)(1) provides that a statement is not hearsay if the declarant testifies at the trial or hearing and is subject to cross-examination concerning the statement, and the statement is:

      1) Inconsistent with the declarant's testimony and was given under oath subject to the penalty of perjury at a trial, hearing, or other proceeding, or in a deposition; or

      2) Consistent with the declarant's testimony and is offered to rebut an express or implied charge against the declarant of recent fabrication or improper influence or motive; or

      3) One of identification of a person made after perceiving the person.

   b. **Rationale.** Witnesses sometimes change their testimony over time. Under traditional rules, a witness who originally testifies one way, then testifies another way at trial, could be impeached through cross-examination about the prior inconsistent statement. A prior consistent statement could be used to rebut an express or implied charge against the declarant of recent fabrication or improper influence or motive. The federal rules represent a compromise. Prior inconsistent statements can be used as substantive evidence, but only if in a formal setting.

2. **Prior Inconsistent Statements.**

   a. **Introduction.** A witness who admits making a prior statement and admits that the statement is true simply adopts the statement and there is no hearsay problem. When the witness either denies making the prior statement or denies that the statement was true, traditionally the prior inconsistent statement was admissible only to impeach. It could not be used as substantive evidence. Under the Rule, such statements can now be used as substantive evidence. The rationale is that the dangers of hearsay do not exist when the witness is available for cross-examination. In addition, the prior statement was made closer to the event it describes and therefore has some likelihood of being more truthful than the in-court testimony.

## b.    Scope of "proceeding" requirement--

---

# State v. Smith, 651 P.2d 207 (Wash. 1982).

---

**Facts.** Conlin was assaulted in a motel room. When police arrived, she told them that Smith (D) had done it and she was afraid. They told her they could do nothing unless she was willing to testify in court. Conlin went to the police station and agreed to press charges. She voluntarily gave a sworn written statement in the form of a notarized affidavit describing the assault and identifying D. At trial, Conlin testified about the same facts but claimed that the attacker was Gomez, and that D had come to her aid. She admitted giving the affidavit, but claimed that she had been upset with D over a fight from the previous night. The prosecution offered the affidavit for impeachment purposes and also as substantive evidence as to D's identity as the assailant. The trial court admitted the affidavit, ruling it was not hearsay under the Washington Rule of Evidence equivalent to Federal Rule 801(d)(1)(A) because it was given in a "proceeding." The jury convicted D. The trial court later granted a new trial, concluding the affidavit should not have been admitted because it had not been given in a "proceeding." The State appeals.

**Issue.** Does a voluntary written sworn statement, given to police at the police station, fall within the definition of nonhearsay as a prior statement under Rule 801(d)(1)(A)?

**Held.** Yes. Judgment reversed and verdict reinstated.

♦    The term "other proceeding" in Rule 801(d)(1)(A) includes grand jury proceedings, which was what the rule as originally drafted specified. Courts have extended the definition beyond grand jury proceedings by applying it to immigration investigations.

♦    No court has decided whether police-station interrogations fall within Rule 801(d)(1)(A), but the rule should not be used to always exclude or always admit such affidavits. The key determinant is reliability. Conlin wrote the affidavit in her own words, she attested to it before a notary, under oath and subject to penalty for perjury, and she admitted in court that she made the statement.

♦    Another factor to consider is the original purpose of the affidavit. The police took Conlin's statement as part of the process of determining the existence of probable cause to file charges against D. In this sense, it is comparable to a grand jury statement, which has the same purpose. The statement therefore falls within Rule 801(d)(1)(A). The jury verdict should be reinstated.

---

## 3.    Prior Consistent Statements.

a. **Introduction.** Traditionally, prior consistent statements were admissible only to rebut charges of recent fabrication or undue influence, but now such statements are admissible as substantive evidence.

b. **Prior consistent statements; pre-motive and post-motive--**

---

# Tome v. United States, 513 U.S. 150 (1995).

---

**Facts.** At the trial of Tome (D) for the sexual abuse of his then four-year-old daughter, A.T., the prosecution offered A.T.'s testimony that D had abused her sexually while in his custody. After cross-examination where the defense suggested that A.T.'s testimony was motivated by her desire to live with her mother, the prosecution offered witnesses who reported statements made by A.T., either to the witnesses themselves or in their hearing, that also tended to show sexual abuse. Over D's objection, the trial court admitted the testimony of these witnesses on the theory that these statements rebutted D's impeachment of A.T., as they were consistent with the allegations of abuse. Apparently, no party and no court disagreed that A.T. had made the statements at times after she had acquired a motive to fabricate, if she had. D was convicted. D appealed, arguing that Rule 801(d)(1)(B) did not authorize the receipt in evidence of post-motive consistent statements. The Tenth Circuit affirmed. The Supreme Court granted certiorari.

**Issue.** Are out-of-court consistent statements made after an alleged improper motive arose admissible under Rule 801(d)(1)(B)?

**Held.** No. Reversed and remanded.

♦ The common law rule before the adoption of the Federal Rules of Evidence was that a prior consistent statement introduced to rebut a charge of recent fabrication or improper influence or motive was admissible if the statement had been made before the alleged fabrication, influence, or motive came into being, but it was inadmissible if made afterwards.

♦ The Federal Rule allows prior consistent statements to rebut a charge that the testimony results from an alleged improper motive, but it does not allow such statements merely to bolster the testimony of the witness. Thus, the prior consistent statements must have been made before the alleged motive arose in order to squarely rebut the impeachment.

♦ Nothing in the Advisory Committee Notes following Rule 801(d)(1)(B) suggests that the Rule intended to alter the common law pre-motive requirement. To the contrary, the Advisory Committee Notes generally support the conclusion that the requirement be applied to Rule 801(d)(1)(B).

♦ Policy also supports this interpretation. If the rule were applied to admit post-motive statements, "the whole emphasis of the trial could shift to the out-of-court statements, not the in-court ones." Specifically, the witnesses' out-of-court statements would tend to show that D commited the abuse rather than show that A.T. did not fabricate her testimony.

**Concurrence** (Scalia, J.). The case can be adequately resolved without resort to the Advisory Committee Rules. It is well-established that the common law must be a source of guidance in our interpretation of the Rules.

**Dissent** (Breyer, J., Rehnquist, C.J., O'Connor, Thomas, JJ.). This case involves relevance, not hearsay. The reason for the common law rule was that a prior consistent statement made prior to the time when the motive to lie arose had no relevance to rebut the charge that the in-court testimony was the product of the motive to lie. From a hearsay perspective, the timing of a prior consistent statement is beside the point. The timing may diminish probative force, but it does not diminish reliability. The proper approach would be to interpret the Rules to authorize a court to allow the use of post-motive, prior consistent statements to rebut a charge of recent fabrication or improper influence or motive. If they are admissible for this rehabilitative purpose, they are admissible as substantive evidence as well. The effect on the trial is minimal, anyway, because it merely repeats in-court testimony,

**Comment.** Under subsection (B) of Rule 801(d)(1), as well as under subsections (A) and (C) thereof, evidence of an out-of-court statement is admissible only if the out-of-court declarant is presently available for cross-examination.

---

4. **Prior Statements of Identification.**

   a. **Introduction.** Identifications that are close to the time of the incident tend to be more credible than later identifications, especially more than in-court identifications when it is obvious who the defendant is. However, despite Rule 801(d)(1)(C), which defines certain prior identifications as non-hearsay, a line of cases has held that certain pretrial identifications cannot be used, such as post-indictment lineups where the defendant did not have counsel.

   b. **Admissibility of police artist sketch--**

**State v. Motta**, 659 P.2d 745 (Haw. 1983).

**Facts.** Iwashita was robbed at gunpoint while working as a cashier. A week later she met with a police artist who made a composite sketch based on her description of the robber. A month later, Iwashita picked Motta (D) from a photographic lineup, and a few days later she identified him at a preliminary hearing. She also identified D at trial. The court admitted the composite sketch over D's objection. D was convicted. D appeals, claiming the sketch was hearsay not covered by an exception.

**Issue.** May a police artist's composite sketch be admitted as substantive evidence under the prior identification exception?

**Held.** Yes. Judgment affirmed.

◆ Courts have taken various approaches to police sketches. One is to deem a sketch not hearsay because it is not a statement. Another is to fit a sketch within a common-law hearsay exception, such as the res gestae exception.

◆ The best approach is to treat a sketch as hearsay and apply the prior identification exception under Rule 801(d)(1)(C). The rationale for this exception is that identification made close to the time of the event is more reliable than in-court identification. This exception allows the use of pretrial identifications as substantive proof of identity; it is not limited to use for corroboration.

◆ A sketch may be admitted as prior identification if the declarant testifies at trial and is subject to cross-examination, and the sketch is made based on a statement of identification of a person made after perceiving him. In this case, Iwashita and the police artist testified at trial and were subject to cross-examination. The sketch was properly admitted.

---

## B. ADMISSIONS BY OPPONENT

1. **Introduction.** An admission is any out-of-court statement or conduct by a party to the litigation that is inconsistent with the party's present position. It can include prior statements, admissions in pleadings, or stipulations. Admissions are useful both to impeach the testimony of a party and as substantive evidence. Many courts treat admissions as exceptions to the hearsay rule. Rule 801(d)(2) simply provides that a statement is not hearsay if the statement is offered against a party and is:

   a. The party's own statement, in either an individual or a representative capacity;

   b. A statement of which the party has manifested an adoption or belief in its truth;

   c. A statement by a person authorized by the party to make a statement concerning the subject;

   d. A statement by the party's agent or servant concerning a matter within the scope of the agency or employment, made during the existence of the relationship;

e. A statement by a co-conspirator of a party during the course and in furtherance of the conspiracy.

*Note*: The contents of the statement are considered but are not alone sufficient to establish the declarant's authority under subdivision (C), the agency or employment relationship and scope thereof under subdivision (D), or the existence of the conspiracy and the participation therein of the declarant and the party against whom the statement is offered under subdivision (E).

2. **Individual Admissions.**

a. **General rule.** There are almost no limits to the use of an individual's own admissions, other than the constitutional right against self-incrimination. A separate issue arises when one person's own confession also names someone else. When co-defendants are involved, however, one defendant's statement might be covered by Rule 801(d)(2)(A) if used against the person who spoke, but not if used against a co-party.

b. **Confession by co-defendant--**

## Bruton v. United States, 391 U.S. 123 (1968).

**Facts.** Bruton (D) and Evans were tried in a joint trial for armed robbery. A postal inspector testified that Evans had orally confessed that he and D had committed the robbery. The court admitted the evidence against Evans, but instructed the jury not to consider it in any respect against D. Both Evans and D were convicted. The Eighth Circuit reversed Evans's conviction, holding that his confession was not admissible against him. However, the court held that the jury instructions protected D adequately. D appeals.

**Issue.** In a joint trial, may a confession made by one co-defendant that includes a statement that his co-defendant also committed the crime be used as evidence against the declarant, so long as the judge instructs the jury not to consider the confession against the co-defendant?

**Held.** No. Judgment reversed.

♦ Although the courts assume that juries follow instructions, there are situations in which an admonition against misuse of evidence is intrinsically ineffective. In such cases, the admonition becomes a "futile collocation of words" and fails its protective purpose.

♦ There are many reasons for conducting joint trials, but each defendant is entitled to confront the witnesses against him and to cross-examine them. The benefits of conducting joint trials do not outweigh these basic constitutional rights.

- In many cases, a limiting instruction may suffice to correct errors such as the admission of inadmissible hearsay. But here, where the incriminating extra-judicial statements of a co-defendant are presented to the jury, limiting instructions are inadequate. This is especially so where Evans himself did not testify, so D had no opportunity to cross-examine him regarding the confession.

---

3. **Adoptive Admissions.**

   a. **Introduction.** A party who knowingly and voluntarily adopts or ratifies another's statement that is inconsistent with the party's trial position may be treated as having admitted the statement. Rule 801(d)(2)(B) simply states that it must be a statement of which the party has manifested an adoption or belief in its truth. The question often arises as to what constitutes a manifestation.

   b. **Silence.** A party's silence or evasion may be treated as a manifestation of adoption or belief in the truth of another's statement. This typically occurs when the party fails to respond to statements made in his presence that a reasonable person in such a position would have unequivocally denied. Three basic requirements apply.

      1) **Comprehension.** The party must have been present and capable of hearing and understanding the statement or accusation.

      2) **Capable of denying.** The party must have been physically and mentally capable of denying the statement.

      3) **Motive.** The party must have had an opportunity and a motive to deny, such that a reasonable person would have denied the statement.

   c. **Criminal cases.** The privilege against self-incrimination prevents the prosecution from using a defendant's refusal to answer questions as an admission of guilt.

   d. **Silence when an objection would be expected--**

---

**United States v. Hoosier**, 542 F.2d 687 (6th Cir. 1976).

---

**Facts.** Hoosier (D) was convicted of armed bank robbery based on the testimony of five witnesses. The fifth witness, Rogers, had been with D before and after the bank robbery. D told Rogers ahead of time that he intended to rob a bank. Three weeks after the robbery, Rogers was with D and D's girlfriend. Rogers testified that D's girlfriend referred to "sacks of money" they had at the hotel. D appeals the conviction, claiming Rogers's testimony was inadmissible hearsay.

**Issue.** May one's silence when an incriminating statement is made constitute an adoption of the statement?

**Held.** Yes. Judgment affirmed.

♦ Because D had previously told Rogers of his plan to rob a bank, D apparently trusted Rogers and D's silence in response to his girlfriend's statement was not due to fear that the statement might be used against him.

♦ Under the circumstances, a person hearing such a statement would probably have denied it if it was not true. These circumstances constituted more than D's mere presence and silence.

---

e. **Post-*Miranda* warning silence--**

## Doyle v. Ohio, 426 U.S. 610 (1976).

**Facts.** Doyle (D) and Wood were prosecuted separately for selling marijuana to Bonnell, an informant. According to Bonnell, he met D and Wood in a bar and drove off with Wood while D left to get the marijuana. The groups later met again. Agents observed Bonnell standing next to D's car with a package. After Bonnell left, D and Wood drove around looking for him. When they were stopped by the police, they had $1,320 that Bonnell apparently received from agents to buy the marijuana. In defense, Wood claimed that he and D had planned to buy marijuana from Bonnell, but changed their minds. He further claimed that Bonnell got mad and threw the money into D's car, after which D and Wood looked for him to find out why he had thrown the money into D's car. At his trial, Wood testified to this version of the deal. On cross-examination, Wood admitted that he did not tell the police what happened when they arrived on the scene. Wood was convicted. The Supreme Court granted certiorari to consider the claim that Wood's silence after being read his *Miranda* warning at the scene could not be used to impeach his testimony.

**Issue.** May a defendant's post-*Miranda* warning silence be used against him on cross-examination for impeachment purposes if he testifies at trial?

**Held.** No. Judgment reversed.

♦ The prosecution claims that a discrepancy between an exculpatory story at trial and silence at the time of arrest gives rise to an inference that the story was fabricated after the arrest to conform to the prosecution's evidence.

♦ While cross-examination is important, a defendant's silence after receiving a *Miranda* warning may be nothing more than his exercise of the *Miranda* rights.

Such post-arrest silence is insolubly ambiguous. Accordingly, use for impeachment purposes of a defendant's silence at the time of arrest and after receiving *Miranda* warnings violates the Due Process Clause of the Fourteenth Amendment.

**Dissent** (Stevens, Blackmun, Rehnquist, JJ.). Ds in these cases did not rely on the *Miranda* warning as an explanation for why they remained silent, so the due process rationale is inapplicable here. The prosecution should be permitted to use silence to comment on the lack of credibility of Wood, but not to claim that his silence is inconsistent with his innocence.

―――――――――

4.  **Admissions by Employees and Agents.**

    a.  **Introduction.** Admissions by agents and employees may be binding against the employer as long as:

        1)  The agency is proved by evidence other than the hearsay statement;

        2)  The admissions relate to current matters; and

        3)  The admissions were made within the scope of the agent's authority.

    b.  **No requirement of personal knowledge--**

**Mahlandt v. Wild Canid Survival & Research Center, Inc.,** 588 F.2d 626 (8th Cir. 1978).

**Facts.** Poos, an employee of Wild Canid Survival & Research Center, Inc. (D), kept a wolf in his yard in connection with his job. The wolf had been raised in a children's zoo and had been known to be very gentle. Mahlandt (P), who was under four years old, was seen walking next to Poos's residence. The next thing anyone saw was P lying on the ground inside Poos's yard near the wolf and crying. He had several lacerations, abrasions, and bruises. When Poos found out about the incident, he left a note on the door of D's president stating that the wolf "bit a child that came in our backyard." He later spoke with the president and told him that the wolf had bitten the child. Additionally, the matter was recorded in the minutes of D's directors' meeting. Other evidence indicated that P was most likely injured by crawling under the fence, not by the wolf. At trial, the court excluded Poos's admissions in the note, the statement, and the minutes because Poos had no personal knowledge of the facts. The jury found for D and P appeals.

**Issue.** To introduce an agent's admissions, must the proponent show that the declarant had personal knowledge of the facts underlying the statement?

**Held.** No. Judgment reversed.

♦ As far as Poos is concerned, the note and the statement were not hearsay because they were his own statements, which he believed to be true.

♦ Under Federal Rule 801(d)(2)(D), Poos's statements are admissible against D as admissions of an agent. There is no requirement that Poos have had personal knowledge of the facts. Although some commentators argue for such a requirement, it does not at present exist. Furthermore, it is inconsequential that the admissions were made "in-house" rather than to a third party.

♦ The board minutes could not be used against Poos because there was no agency relationship with Poos to justify admission. They could be admissible against D, but this limited use, plus the repetitive nature of the minutes and their low probative value, supports the trial court's ruling on this issue.

**Comment.** The policy behind not requiring personal knowledge is that a party will not make statements against interest unless satisfied that the statements are true. Thus, an admission may be based solely on hearsay.

---

5. **Co-conspirators.** Statements made by one co-conspirator may be used against the other conspirators as long as the prerequisites are met.

   a. **Conspiracy established.** The conspiracy in which the defendant was involved must be established. Traditionally, this had to be by independent evidence, but the trend is to permit use of the statements themselves to prove the conspiracy.

   b. **During conspiracy.** The statement must have been made during the conspiracy.

   c. **In furtherance of conspiracy.** The statement must have been made in furtherance of the conspiracy. A mere narration does not qualify; it must be a statement intended to further the objectives of the conspiracy.

   d. **Use of co-conspirator's statement to prove conspiracy--**

**Bourjaily v. United States**, 483 U.S. 171 (1987).

**Facts.** Greathouse was an informant for the FBI. He arranged to sell cocaine to Lonardo, who in turn agreed to find someone to distribute the cocaine. Lonardo recruited his "friend," Bourjaily (D).Their conversations were recorded. During one conversation, D asked Greathouse about the price and quality of the cocaine. In a later conversation, Greathouse and Lonardo agreed to meet at a particular hotel parking lot, where Lonardo would take the cocaine and give it to D, who would be parked in his own car. When the transaction took place, FBI agents arrested Lonardo and D, who was waiting in the parked car in which Lonardo had placed the cocaine. There was over $20,000 in cash in D's car as well. D was charged with possession of cocaine with intent to distribute and with conspiring to distribute cocaine. The trial court permitted the prosecution to use Lonardo's telephone statements about his friend, on the ground that these statements, plus the actual events in the parking lot, established a conspiracy between Lonardo and D and that the statements were thus made in the course of and in furtherance of the conspiracy. Lonardo himself did not testify at trial. D was convicted. The court of appeals upheld the conviction. The Supreme Court granted certiorari.

**Issue.** In determining whether a conspiracy existed to make admissible a declarant's statements involving an accused, may the court consider the statements themselves as proof of the conspiracy?

**Held.** Yes. Judgment affirmed.

- ♦ Under Federal Rule 801(d)(2)(E), the statement of a co-conspirator is not hearsay when offered against a party who is a co-conspirator if it was made during the course and in furtherance of the conspiracy. A court must determine as a preliminary question that the statement falls within the rule before it is admitted. Such preliminary questions are decided by the court under Rule 104(a), and must he proved by the offering party by a preponderance of the evidence.

- ♦ D claims that, under *Glasser v. United States,* 315 U.S. 60 (1942), the court that makes the preliminary factual determination may not rely on the statements themselves. This "bootstrapping" rule has been followed by the courts of appeal. However, the Federal Rules of Evidence were adopted after the *Glasser* case. Under Rule 104(a), a court is not bound by the rules of evidence, except privileges, when it makes preliminary factual determinations regarding the admissibility of evidence.

- ♦ D asserts that the bootstrapping rule survives Rule 104, but the meaning of Rule 104 is plain: it permits the trial court to consider any evidence whatsoever, subject to privilege. The rule prevails over the *Glasser* bootstrapping rule. This does not mean that hearsay statements may be admitted without credible proof of the conspiracy. The statements themselves may be such credible proof, especially when corroborated by independent evidence. In this case, D's conduct corroborated the statements of Lonardo regarding his "friend." When all the evidence is considered together, the evidence supports the court's determination that a conspiracy existed.

- ♦ D claims the Confrontation Clause prevents use of Lonardo's statements because Lonardo did not testify at trial. However, the Confrontation Clause is not interpreted literally; its concern with limiting evidence usable against an accused must be balanced with society's interest in accurate fact finding. As a general rule, the prosecution must demonstrate both the declarant's unavailability and indicia of reliability pertaining to the out-of-court declaration. Neither of these are constitutional requirements, however. The co-conspirator exception to the hearsay rule has a long tradition, and the Constitution does not require an independent inquiry of reliability once the requirements of Rule 801(d)(2)(E) are met.

**Dissent** (Blackmun, Brennan, Marshall, JJ.).

♦    The Court has decided that the common law requirement that a conspiracy be shown from independent evidence had been changed by adoption of the Federal Rules of Evidence. This approach ignores the foundation for the co-conspirator exemption—that such statements are admissible based on agency principles, not because of any particular guarantees of reliability. The agency concept is the reason that statements, to be admissible, must be made in furtherance of the conspiracy. It is also the reason why independent evidence is required; *i.e.,* an agent's statements may not be used by themselves to prove the existence of the agency relationship. Congress retained the agency rationale and thus intended to maintain the common law approach. The statement itself should not be considered when the court makes its preliminary factual determination under Rule 104(a).

♦    The Court's pragmatic approach to reliability indicates that if a co-conspirator's statements are corroborated, the trial court may determine whether the statements are sufficiently reliable. However, the common law rule is the result of long experience and recognizes the unreliability of such statements. Permitting the trial court to consider the statements themselves in determining whether a conspiracy existed has the potential to transform a series of innocuous actions into evidence that the defendant was participating in a criminal conspiracy. At least the Court does not decide that no corroboration is required.

♦    The Confrontation Clause requires some indicia of reliability of the out-of-court statement before it may be admitted. Since the co-conspiracy exception is not based on reliability, but instead on agency principles, the fact that it is a long-standing exception does not provide any indicia of reliability. The Court answers the Confrontation Clause challenge by noting that the exception has traditionally been allowed, yet it removes from the exemption one of the few safeguards against unreliability that it possesses—the requirement that the conspiracy be proved by independent evidence.

## C.  UNRESTRICTED EXCEPTIONS

### 1.    Present Sense Impressions and Excited Utterances.

a. **Introduction.** Because of the spontaneous nature of the utterance, two types of statements are not excluded by the hearsay rule even when the declarant is available as a witness. They are described in Rule 803(1) and (2).

   1) **Rule 803(1) present sense impression.** A statement describing or explaining an event or condition made while the declarant was perceiving the event or condition, or immediately thereafter, is a present sense impression.

   2) **Rule 803(2) excited utterance.** A statement relating to a startling event or condition made while the declarant was under the stress of excitement caused by the event or condition is an excited utterance.

b. **Present sense impression--**

---

## Nuttal v. Reading Co., 235 F.2d 546 (3rd Cir. 1956).

---

**Facts.** Nuttal (P) sued Reading Co. (D), claiming that D was liable for P's husband's death because he was forced to work when he was too sick to perform his duties. P won the first trial, but the judge ordered a new trial. In the second trial, the judge refused to admit affidavits by co-workers and refused to allow P or a co-worker to testify about P's husband's statements regarding his illness. P wanted to testify about her husband's telephone conversation with D on the morning before he went to work. Her husband told D that he was very sick and did not feel he could make it to work, but D required him to go to work anyway. The court directed a verdict for D. P appeals.

**Issue.** Does the present sense impression exception apply to a witness's testimony about one side of an out-of-court declarant's telephone conversation?

**Held.** Yes. Judgment reversed.

♦ The conversation P wanted to testify about tends to show that P's husband was being forced to work by D's employee who was P's husband's supervisor.

♦ Although P did not hear the supervisor's statements, her husband's characterization of those statements was made at the time he heard them. Being contemporaneous, these characterizations are free from the possibility of lapse of memory and are unlikely to be the product of conscious misrepresentation.

♦ The court should have admitted P's testimony about the conversation. Because this testimony goes to the heart of the case, refusal to admit it was reversible error.

---

## c. Excited utterance--

## United States v. Iron Shell, 633 F.2d 77 (8th Cir. 1980).

**Facts.** Iron Shell (D) had been drinking heavily when he left the house where he was staying to go to his mother's house. Along the trail, he approached Lucy, a nine-year-old girl. D grabbed Lucy and pulled her down into some bushes. One witness heard Lucy scream. Another witness who responded saw D lying next to Lucy, who was crying and had her jeans down to her ankles. D ran away, and another witness, Lunderman, saw Lucy come out of the bushes pulling up her pants. Lucy told Lunderman "that guy tried to take my pants off." Lunderman took Lucy to the police station, and then to the magistrate's office, where Officer Marshall asked Lucy "What happened?" Lucy responded that D grabbed her, held her around the neck, and told her to be quiet. She further stated that he pulled her pants down and put his hands between her legs. This interview took place about an hour after the assault. D was charged with assault with intent to commit rape. The court allowed Marshall to testify about what Lucy said at the interview. D was convicted. D appeals, claiming Marshall's testimony was hearsay that was not within any exceptions.

**Issue.** May a statement fall within the excited utterance exception if it is made an hour after the event and in response to an inquiry?

**Held.** Yes. Judgment affirmed.

♦ Rule 803(2) allows admission of hearsay if it is a "statement relating to a startling event or condition made while the declarant was under the stress of excitement caused by the event or condition." D claims that Lucy's statement could not fall within this exception because when she made the statement, Lucy was quiet and not crying and she had not made any spontaneous statements since immediately following the assault.

♦ The lapse of time between the startling event and the out-of-court statement is relevant but not dispositive. Other relevant factors are the age of the declarant, her physical and mental condition, the characteristics of the event, and the subject matter of the statements. The key issue is whether the statement was spontaneous, excited, or impulsive rather than the product of reflection and deliberation.

♦ In this case, it is clear that Lucy was nervous and scared. An assault such as this would create substantial stress and fear for a young girl. Marshall merely asked Lucy "What happened?" This is not a leading question and would not destroy the excitement required for application of the exception.

♦ The trial court could reasonably find, given Lucy's age, the surprise of the assault and its shocking nature, that Lucy was still under the stress of the attack when she spoke with Marshall; *i.e.*, that she was in a state of continuous excitement from the time of the assault through the time she made the statement.

---

## 2. State of Mind.

### a. Introduction.

1) **Then-existing physical condition.** A person's spontaneous statements about sensation or bodily condition, made at the time of the condition, are admissible to prove the condition. [Fed. R. Evid. 803(3)] However, most courts do not allow out-of-court statements about how the declarant felt in the past. Rule 803(4) allows statements of past physical condition when made for the purpose of medical diagnosis or treatment.

2) **Then-existing mental or emotional condition.**

   a) **Present mental state.** If a person's state of mind at a particular time is at issue, contemporaneous declarations showing the state of mind are admissible. This hearsay exception applies to the declarant's intent, motive, plan, emotions, confusion, knowledge, etc.

   b) **Present intent to prove subsequent conduct.** Declarations of present state of mind may also be admitted to show the probability that the declarant did a subsequent act pursuant to the declared state of mind. [Fed. R. Evid. 803(3)] For instance, a decedent's declaration of his intent to commit suicide would be admissible when the issue is whether he was murdered or took his own life.

   c) **Past state of mind.** Declarations about a past state of mind are not normally admissible. One exception is when the issue involves the execution or interpretation of the declarant's will.

### b. Evidence of intent admissible to prove act--

---

## Mutual Life Insurance Co. v. Hillmon, 145 U.S. 285 (1892).

---

**Facts.** Hillmon (P), wife of John Hillmon, brought suit against Mutual Life Insurance Co. (D) and other insurers of the life of John Hillmon. At trial, D claimed that the alleged body of John Hillmon was actually that of Walters. P's evidence tended to show that the body was Hillmon's. D sought to introduce letters written by Walters in which Walters stated his intention to accompany Hillmon to the place where the body was later found, which would corroborate D's other evidence. The trial court refused to admit the letters and found for P. D appeals.

**Issue.** May evidence of an out-of-court declarant's intentions be admitted to prove the declarant did what was intended?

**Held.** Yes. Judgment reversed.

♦ When a person's intent is a distinct and material fact in a chain of circumstances, it is provable by that person's contemporaneous oral or written declaration. The letters were competent to prove that Walters had the intent to go with Hillman.

♦ Such evidence is more trustworthy than the declarant's own memory of his former state of mind, especially when it is written, as it was in this case.

♦ Once Walters's intent to go is shown, the intent can be used to infer that it was likely Walters acted in accordance with his intent.

---

c.    **Intent to do something with another person--**

---

**United States v. Pheaster.** 544 F.2d 353 (9th Cir. 1976).

---

**Facts.** Pheaster and others (Ds) were charged with conspiracy to kidnap Adell. Adell disappeared after leaving some friends in a restaurant. At the trial, two of Adell's friends testified over Ds' objections that Adell had told them he was going to meet Angelo, one of the defendants, outside the restaurant and that he said he would be right back. The court allowed the testimony only to show Adell's state of mind and not for the truth or falsity of the statement. Ds were convicted. Ds appeal.

**Issue.** May "state of mind" hearsay be admitted when it reveals the declarant's intent to do something with another person?

**Held.** Yes. Judgment affirmed.

♦ The statements are undoubtedly relevant to show Adell did not voluntarily disappear, but if admitted for that reason alone, they would be unduly prejudicial to Angelo, who was specifically named. If the statements could be used to show that Adell did meet Angelo, then they would certainly be admissible.

♦ The *Hillmon* doctrine states that when the performance of a particular act by a person is an issue in a case, his intention to do the act may be shown. The jury may infer from the intention that the act was performed. Ds claim the *Hillmon* doctrine should not be extended to situations where the intention involves another person.

♦ Adell's statements really included two separate intentions: his own and Angelo's. The statement of Angelo's intentions has nothing to do with the declarant's state of mind and could not normally be admitted because no hearsay exception applies to such statements. Despite this criticism of the *Hillmon* doctrine, it has been widely applied to situations such as this one, as long as the declarant is unavailable and the testimony is relevant and trustworthy. Because these conditions were satisfied here, there was no error.

---

3.  **Statements to Physicians.**

    a.  **Introduction.** Rule 803(4) excludes from the hearsay rule "Statements made for purposes of medical diagnosis or treatment and describing medical history, or past or present symptoms, pain, or sensations, or the inception or general character of the cause or external source thereof insofar as reasonably pertinent to diagnosis or treatment."

    b.  **Rationale.** A patient seeking medical diagnosis and treatment has a strong motivation to be truthful. The same guarantee of trustworthiness applies to statements about causation that are reasonably pertinent to the same purposes.

    c.  **Identifying abuser to physician--**

---

**Blake v. State**, 933 P.2d 474 (Wyo. 1997).

---

**Facts.** The 16-year-old victim of alleged sexual abuse was taken from her high school to a hospital emergency room for examination. During the examination, Dr. Bowers asked her questions about the abuse. The girl responded by identifying Blake (D), her stepfather, as the perpetrator. Bowers testified at D's trial about the girl's statements. D was convicted. D appeals, claiming Bowers's testimony about identity did not fall within the Wyoming Rule of Evidence identical to Rule 803(4).

**Issue.** If a child victim of sexual abuse identifies the perpetrator during a medical examination, may the attending physician relate the statement in court as evidence of identity?

**Held.** Yes. Judgment affirmed.

♦ The general rule does not allow statements attributing fault or identity to be introduced as evidence. However, there is an exception to this rule in situations involving physical or sexual abuse of children because of the special character of diagnosis and treatment in sexual abuse cases.

♦ Courts should apply a two-part test in this type of case. First, the declarant's motive in making the statement must be consistent with the purposes of promoting treatment or diagnosis. Second, the content of the statement must be reasonably relied on by a physician in treatment or diagnosis.

♦ At trial, Dr. Bowers testified that in performing a rape kit examination, she takes a history from the patient about what happened so she can properly use the kit and provide appropriate medical care. She said it is important for her to know the victim's emotional state, and that knowing the assailant's identity frequently determines the extent to which testing and treatment is given.

♦ Dr. Bowers's testimony satisfied the two-part test. Therefore, her testimony about the victim's identification of D falls within the hearsay exception for statements given for purposes of medical diagnosis or treatment.

---

### 4. Past Recollection Recorded.

    **a. Introduction.** Rule 803(5) excludes from the hearsay rule "A memorandum or record concerning a matter about which a witness once had knowledge but now has insufficient recollection to enable the witness to testify fully and accurately, shown to have been made or adopted by the witness when the matter was fresh in the witness'[s] memory and to reflect that knowledge correctly. If admitted, the memorandum or record may be read into evidence but may not itself be received as an exhibit unless offered by an adverse party."

    **b. Rationale.** There is a guarantee of trustworthiness where a record is made while the events are still fresh in mind. Some courts, including federal courts, require that the witness have some degree of impaired memory before this type of evidence may be used to protect against having people prepare such statements for purposes of litigation.

    **c. Impaired memory--**

---

## Ohio v. Scott, 285 N.E.2d 344 (Ohio 1972).

---

**Facts.** Tackett, a friend of Scott (D), had a conversation with D at a theater shortly before D was arrested for shooting offenses. The next day, Tackett gave the police a handwritten, signed statement about her conversation with D. In her statement, Tackett said that D had been drinking, and that he told her he had wrecked a car and had shot a guy. She stated that he asked her for help, but she ran out of the theater and left in a car.

D was charged with shooting at another with intent to kill, wound, or maim. At D's trial, Tackett was called as a witness, but she said she could not recall exactly what D said during their conversation, other than he said something about somebody being shot. The prosecutor presented to Tackett her previous handwritten statement. Tackett verified that she had written the statement, that it contained what she had remembered at the time she made it, and that it was true. She also said her memory was better at the time she gave the handwritten statement than it was at the time of the trial. D was convicted. D appeals, claiming Tackett's previous statement should not have been admitted into evidence.

**Issue.** May an out-of-court statement made by a witness testifying in court be used as evidence where the witness's memory was better at the time she made the statement than it was at trial?

**Held.** Yes. Judgment affirmed.

♦ The rule of "past recollection recorded" has not been previously recognized in Ohio. The concept is an offshoot from the practice of allowing a witness to refresh her memory by examining her own written memorandum, called "present recollection refreshed." The two concepts are legally different.

♦ In a situation of "present recollection refreshed," the witness testifies from present, independent knowledge, using the memorandum merely to refresh her memory. In the "past recollection recorded" situation, the witness testifies that her present memory is not as good as it was at the time she wrote the memorandum, and that the recollection recorded in the memorandum was accurate.

♦ The doctrine of "past recollection recorded" is based on sound logic and should be adopted in Ohio. To fit within the exception: (i) the statement must consist of facts of which the witness has firsthand knowledge; (ii) it must be the original memorandum made near the time of the event while the witness had a clear and accurate memory of it; (iii) the witness must lack a present recollection of the details of the event; and (iv) the witness must state that the memorandum was accurate.

♦ Each of the elements was satisfied in this case. D has no valid constitutional objection, as the United States Supreme Court has previously held that use of statements of past recollection recorded does not violate the Confrontation Clause.

**Dissent.** The written statement should not be admitted because it was not made in D's presence. As written evidence, it will go with the jury into deliberations and thereby acquire undue weight. In this case, the prosecution did not even attempt to refresh Tackett's recollection as is required by the traditional formulation of the rule.

5. **Business Records.**

    a. **Introduction.** Business records are admissible as exceptions to the hearsay rule.

        1) **General requirements.**

            a) **Regular course of business.** Business records generally are admissible when the sources of information and the time and method of preparation indicate that they are trustworthy. Such records can be used to prove the occurrence or nonoccurrence of a transaction. [Fed. R. Evid. 803(7)] There are several factors to consider in assessing admissibility.

                (1) **Regular course of business defined.** The definition of "business" is broad enough to include most organizations, including hospitals, churches, and schools. [Fed. R. Evid, 803(6)] The records must be prepared in the regular course of the activity of the business.

                    (a) The entry must be made by someone whose employment duty required him to make such entries.

                    (b) The records must be of a type customarily kept by the business as part of its primary activities.

            b) **Personal knowledge.** The source of the information must be someone with personal knowledge; however, the person making the entry need not have personal knowledge.

            c) **Contemporaneity.** Entries must be made at or near the time of the event recorded.

            d) **Foundation testimony.** A custodian of the records, but not necessarily the entrant, must authenticate the records by identifying them and testifying as to their method of preparation and safekeeping.

    b. **Adequacy of information in medical records--**

---

**Petrocelli v. Gallison**, 679 F.2d 286 (1st Cir. 1982).

---

**Facts.** Dr. Gallison (D) performed hernia surgery on Petrocelli (P). P suffered intense pain after the surgery. After several months, he consulted Dr. Swartz who performed a second hernia surgery. P ultimately had a third operation as well, still suffering pain. P sued D for malpractice. At trial, P's wife testified that during a phone conversation she had with D after the first surgery, D told her that he had cut a nerve. D denied that he had severed a nerve. P sought to introduce a report filed by Dr. Swartz the day after he performed P's second operation. The "Indications" section of the report stated that P's nerve was severed, but the "Procedure" section did not mention the nerve. P also sought to introduce part of another medical record describing P's pain from a transected nerve. The court refused to admit the evidence. The jury found for D. P appeals.

**Issue.** May a business record be admitted under Rule 803(6) if the source of the information contained within the record is not readily ascertainable?

**Held.** No. Judgment affirmed.

♦ Rule 803(6), the business records exception, covers reports of opinions and diagnoses that are made at or near the time by a person with knowledge, so long as they are kept in the regular course of business. P claims the medical records fit within this exception.

♦ The problem with the reports in this case is that they do not indicate where the information came from. The statements themselves were insufficiently detailed to reveal whether the doctors had made an independent determination. If the information was merely a notation of what P or his wife told the reporting physicians, the exception would not apply. A hospital patient relating his own history is not part of the hospital's "business" routine that the business records exception requires.

♦ Admitting this type of evidence could allow a jury to misconstrue the statements as definitive opinion testimony on the most critical issue of the case. P did not offer any corroborative evidence to assure the court that the statements were professional opinions. Given that the records would be admitted for their truth without any opportunity to cross-examine the physicians who made them, the court did not err in excluding them.

♦ P might have sought to introduce the records under Rule 803(4) as medical records, but P did not argue that he or his wife made the statements. The records could not otherwise be considered patient history. If P had made the statements, the records would have served merely as corroboration of P's testimony and not as medical opinion.

---

c. **Source of information--**

---

**Norcon, Inc. v. Kotowski,** 971 P.2d 158 (Alaska 1999).

---

**Facts.** Kotowski (P) worked for Norcon, Inc. (D) which had a contract to perform services as part of the cleanup from the Exxon Valdez oil spill. P was sexually harassed by her supervisor, Posehn. D's investigators told P that Posehn was under investigation and asked P to wear a microphone to record conversations at a party in Posehn's room. During the party, P drank alcohol. P and Posehn were fired a short time later. Posehn was fired for his sexual relationship with another employee of D's. P was fired for drinking. P sued D for sexual harassment and emotional distress. At trial, the court admitted a memo (the Ford memo) written by Ford and other investigators employed by another company who interviewed D's employees. Ford was looking into allegations of rule breaking and gathered information about P, Posehn, and other employees of D. The memo included statements from D's employees to the effect that Posehn had many female visitors in his room and that he used alcohol as a means to starting sexual activity with females under his supervision. P won about $10,300 in actual damages and $3.8 million in punitive damages (although this was later reduced to $500,000). D appeals, claiming the judge improperly admitted the memo.

**Issue.** May investigative memos containing statements made by D's own employees be admitted into evidence as admissions of a party-opponent?

**Held.** Yes. Judgment affirmed.

♦        D claims that Rule 803(6) does not apply to the Ford memo because, even if Ford acted within the regular course of business when he prepared the memo, there was no proof that the informants were acting within the regular course of their business.

♦        The key to the business record exception is that all participants act routinely, under a duty of accuracy, with employer reliance on the result. If the supplier of the information is not acting in the regular course of business, an essential link is broken and the assurance of accuracy does not extend to the information itself. Therefore, the business record exception does not apply as to the statements of the informants.

♦        P argues alternatively that the information in the Ford memo should be regarded as nonhearsay admissions of a party-opponent under Rule 801(d)(2). D has not contested the admissibility of the memo on this theory. Because the informants who gave information to Ford were employees of D and were acting as D's agents, and as supervisors they were required to report violations, their statements were properly admitted.

**Comment.** The Ford memo was admissible under Rule 803(6), but the court also relies on the admission by a party-opponent under Rule 801(d)(2) to allow use of the informants' statements as proof of what the statements assert. Note that a company's own accident investigation report is not admissible under Rule 803(6) because such reports are not for the systematic conduct of the business, but are intended for use in courts for litigating. To allow a company to use such reports would open the door to avoidance of cross-examination of the company's employees who made the reports. [*See* Palmer v. Hoffman, 318 U.S. 109 (1943).]

### 6. Public Records.

a. **Introduction.** Rule 803(8) excludes from hearsay

> Records, reports, statements, or data compilations, in any form, of public offices or agencies, setting forth (A) the activities of the office or agency, or (B) matters observed pursuant to duty imposed by law as to which matters there was a duty to report, excluding, however, in criminal cases matters observed by police officers and other law enforcement personnel, or (C) in civil actions and proceedings and against the Government in criminal cases, factual findings resulting from an investigation made pursuant to authority granted by law, unless the sources of information or other circumstances indicate lack of trustworthiness.

b. **Fault attributed in patrolman's report--**

---

**Baker v. Elcona Homes Corp.,** 588 F.2d 551 (6th Cir. 1978, *cert. denied*, 441 U.S. 933 (1979).

---

**Facts.** Baker (P) was one of six people in a car traveling on S.R. 4, a two-lane highway. At the intersection with U.S. 20, a four-lane divided highway, P's car collided with a semi-tractor truck traveling on the divided highway. P was the only survivor in the car. P was seriously injured and could not remember anything about the collision. Slabach, the driver of the truck, was returning home from making a delivery for Elcona Homes Corp. (D), his employer. Slabach was acting in the course of his employment. At trial, Slabach testified that he was blinded by the sun and could not see the traffic light. D called Sgt. Hendrickson, the patrolman who responded six minutes after the accident, to testify about the accident scene. After his testimony, D offered into evidence Hendrickson's accident report. P objected, but the court admitted it into evidence. The report contained a statement that P's car apparently ran a red light, and also indicated that the failure of P's car to yield the right of way and the preoccupation of both drivers were contributing factors. The report also contained a statement made by Slabach. The jury found for D. P appeals.

**Issue.** May a traffic accident report that attributes fault be admitted as a public record under Rule 803(8)?

**Held.** Yes. Judgment affirmed.

◆ The trial court apparently admitted the report as a recorded recollection under Rule 803(5), but this was a mistake because it's not clear that Hendrickson had insufficient recollection under that rule, and because Hendrickson was not an adverse party to D, since D called him as a witness.

♦ However, the observation portion of the report qualifies as a public record under Rule 803(8)(B) because Hendrickson recorded his direct observations made in the course of his investigation. He had a legal duty to conduct the investigation.

♦ Slabach's statements and Hendrickson's findings about the right-of-way are admissible if they are "factual findings" within the meaning of Rule 803(8)(C). The rule allows admission of factual findings made by the preparer of the report from disputed evidence, subject to considerations of trustworthiness.

♦ The factors to determine whether there is a lack of trustworthiness include: (i) the timeliness of the investigation; (ii) the special skill or experience of the official; (iii) whether a hearing was held; and (iv) possible motivational problems. The trial court did not make a finding on trustworthiness because it did not rely on Rule 803(8), but P had the burden to show a lack of trustworthiness. P did not meet this burden.

♦ Hendrickson arrived at the scene within minutes of the accident and began his investigation immediately. He had 28 years of experience and had investigated many accidents before. There was no hearing held, but this is not a requirement. Hendrickson conducted a thorough, impartial investigation without any improper motive. Consequently, his findings of fact were properly admitted.

♦ P also objects to the admission of Slabach's statement contained in the report. Although the statement was not an official observation or fact finding, it was not hearsay because under Rule 801(d)(1)(B), it was consistent with Slabach's testimony. At trial, P extensively cross-examined Slabach, and it was therefore proper to allow the statement in the report to rebut P's claim that Slabach's testimony was not a recent fabrication or result of an improper influence or motive.

**Comment.** Some states have modified this rule to exclude police reports from the exception. Some court decisions also exclude police reports based on eyewitness statements.

---

### c. Evaluative and law enforcement reports in criminal cases--

## United States v. Oates, 560 F.2d 45 (2d Cir. 1977).

**Facts.** Oates (D) was convicted of possession of heroin with intent to distribute. The evidence against D included the testimony of a government witness who identified a written chemist's report prepared by Mr. Weinberg, a Customs Service chemist who could not be at trial because of illness. The judge permitted the witness, also a Customs Service chemist, to identify Weinberg's signature on the report, which identified the substance seized from D as heroin. The document was then admitted and given to the jury. D appeals.

**Issue.** Is it error to permit the introduction of a government report and analysis identifying a substance seized in a criminal investigation without opportunity of cross-examination?

**Held.** Yes. Judgment reversed.

♦ The report and worksheet of the chemist were written assertions offered to prove the truth of the matters asserted in them. They do not fall within the business records exception because they are law enforcement reports that do not qualify for admission under Rule 803(8)(B) and (C). Allowing such evidence would counteract the requirements of the public records exception.

♦ The documents cannot qualify as public records and reports because they were prepared by law enforcement personnel in connection with an investigation. In such cases, the accused's right to confront the preparer of the document is paramount.

---

## D. EXCEPTION WHEN DECLARANT UNAVAILABLE

### 1. The Unavailability Requirement.

**a. Introduction.** Rule 804 sets forth hearsay exceptions that apply only when the declarant is unavailable as a witness.

**b. Unavailability.** There are only certain types of unavailability that qualify under Rule 804. "Unavailability as a witness" under Rule 804(a) includes situations in which the declarant:

1) Is exempted by ruling of the court on the ground of privilege from testifying concerning the subject matter of the declarant's statement;

2) Persists in refusing to testify concerning the subject matter of the declarant's statement despite an order of the court to do so;

3) Testifies to a lack of memory of the subject matter of the declarant's statement;

4) Is unable to be present or to testify at the hearing because of death or then existing physical or mental illness or infirmity; or

5)  Is absent from the hearing and the proponent of a statement has been unable to procure the declarant's attendance or testimony by process or other reasonable means.

c.  **Caveat.** Rule 804(a) also provides that: "A declarant is not unavailable as a witness if exemption, refusal, claim of lack of memory, inability, or absence is due to the procurement or wrongdoing of the proponent of a statement for the purpose of preventing the witness from attending or testifying."

d.  **Prosecution's duty to use efforts to make witness available--**

## Barber v. Page, 390 U.S. 719 (1968).

**Facts.** Barber (D) was charged by Oklahoma state officials with armed robbery. At a preliminary hearing, D and a co-defendant, Woods, were represented by one lawyer, Parks. Woods waived his right against self-incrimination, and Parks withdrew from representing him. Woods's testimony incriminated D and Parks did not cross-examine Woods. By the time of D's trial, Woods was in federal prison in Texas. The prosecution introduced a transcript of Woods's preliminary hearing testimony. D objected on hearsay grounds, but the court admitted the evidence. D was convicted. He sought habeas corpus relief in federal court. The lower courts denied relief. The Supreme Court granted certiorari.

**Issue.** In a criminal case, may a witness be deemed unavailable if he is incarcerated in another state and the prosecution makes no effort to obtain his presence at trial?

**Held.** No. Judgment reversed.

♦  Traditionally, the courts assumed that the mere absence of a witness from the jurisdiction was sufficient grounds for considering the witness unavailable. This rule is no longer valid because cooperation between the states and between the states and the federal government has improved.

♦  A witness is not "unavailable" for purposes of the exception to the confrontation requirement unless the prosecution has made a good-faith effort to obtain the witness's presence at trial.

♦  D did not waive his right to confront Woods at trial when Parks did not cross-examine Woods at the preliminary hearing. D could not have known then that Woods would be in a federal prison and not be made available at trial. But even had D cross-examined Woods at the preliminary hearing, he would not have waived his right to confrontation at trial.

**Comment.** In 2004, the Court reaffirmed the importance of the Confrontation Clause in *Crawford v. Washington, infra. Crawford* concerns "testimonial" given prior to trial. The decision indicates that cross-examination may satisfy the clause, but the mere opportunity to cross-examine may not suffice. However, after the *Crawford* decision, *Barber* still appears to be good law.

---

2. **Former Testimony Exception.**

    a.   **Introduction.** The first exception for which the declarant must be unavailable is for former testimony. Rule 804(b)(1) provides that:

> Testimony given as a witness at another hearing of the same or a different proceeding, or in a deposition taken in compliance with law in the course of the same or another proceeding, if the party against whom the testimony is now offered, or, in a civil action or proceeding, a predecessor in interest, had an opportunity and similar motive to develop the testimony by direct, cross, or redirect examination.

    b.   **Type of shared legal interest required--**

---

**Lloyd v. American Export Lines, Inc.,** 580 F.2d 1179 (3d Cir. 1978).

---

**Facts.** Alvarez and Lloyd (P) were fellow crew members. They got into a fight and each sustained injuries. P sued American Export Lines, Inc. (D) alleging negligence and unseaworthiness, seeking redress for his injuries. D impleaded Alvarez as a third-party defendant and Alvarez counterclaimed against D. Meanwhile, the Coast Guard conducted a hearing to determine whether to suspend or revoke P's merchant mariner's documents. At that hearing, both P and Alvarez testified under oath about the incident and each was represented by counsel. In the present action, P failed to appear for pre-trial depositions and failed to appear to prosecute his case, despite his attorney's attempts to secure his appearance. As a consequence, Alvarez was the only witness to testify at trial regarding the fight. D sought to introduce excerpts of P's testimony from the Coast Guard proceeding, but the trial court refused to allow it. The trial court found for Alvarez and D appeals.

**Issue.** Must the predecessor in interest under Federal Rule 804(b)(1) have the same legal interest as the person against whom the reported testimony is offered?

**Held.** No. Judgment reversed.

    ♦   The unavailability requirement of Rule 804(a)(5) is satisfied, because P's own counsel was unable to obtain his presence despite the great interest P had in the trial.

    ♦   Under Rule 804(b)(1), a "predecessor in interest" of Alvarez must have taken part in the Coast Guard hearing. This term is not defined by the Rules, although it was adopted instead of the more general requirement of participation by a person with "motive and interest similar" to the party against when the evidence is offered. The concept of "interest" requires that the parties seek to satisfy a common "claim or desire or demand." Alvarez's private interest at trial and the Coast Guard's public interest at the hearing involved the same facts and represented the same basic interest. Although the Coast Guard did not have the same legal interest, it had a sufficiently like motive to satisfy Rule 804(b)(1).

**Concurrence.** The result is correct but it should be reached through Rule 804(b)(5), the catchall exception. To interpret "predecessor in interest" as merely requiring a similar motive renders the "predecessor in interest" requirement of Rule 804(b)(1) meaningless.

---

3. **Dying Declaration.** Rule 804(b)(2) allows for admission of hearsay statements under the following circumstances: "In a prosecution for homicide or in a civil action or proceeding, a statement made by a declarant while believing that the declarant's death was imminent, concerning the cause or circumstances of what the declarant believed to be impending death." Such statements are thought to be trustworthy due to psychological factors compelling the declarant to be truthful and the likelihood that the facts in the statement have recently occurred.

4. **Declarations Against Interest.**

   a. **Introduction.** Rule 804(b)(3) defines the exception for a statement against interest as follows:

   > A statement which was at the time of its making so far contrary to the declarant's pecuniary or proprietary interest, or so far tended to subject the declarant to civil or criminal liability, or to render invalid a claim by the declarant against another, that a reasonable person in the declarant's position would not have made the statement unless believing it to be true. A statement tending to expose the declarant to criminal liability and offered to exculpate the accused is not admissible unless corroborating circumstances clearly indicate the trustworthiness of the statement.

   The trustworthiness of such statements is derived from the belief that a person is unlikely to make a statement harming himself unless it is true.

   b. **Statements that are not self-inculpatory cannot be used against others--**

## Williamson v. United States, 512 U.S. 590 (1994).

**Facts.** Harris was stopped for weaving in traffic, and 19 kilograms of cocaine was found in the trunk of his car. He subsequently made several statements to a DEA agent implicating both himself and Williamson (D). Harris refused to make a written or recorded statement, and refused to testify at D's trial. The trial court admitted against D the statements Harris made to the DEA agent. D was convicted and the Supreme Court ultimately granted certiorari.

**Issue.** May third-party statements that inculpate a defendant be admitted under Rule 804(b)(3) if they do not implicate the declarant?

**Held.** No. Judgment reversed. Remanded to the Court of Appeals to determine whether each of Harris's statements was self-inculpatory.

♦ The term "statement," as used in Rule 804(b)(3), includes only those assertions the declarant thought at the time to be against his interest, and not an entire confession, which may contain both self-inculpatory and self-exculpatory declarations.

♦ The principle is based on the assumption that reasonable people, even reasonable people who are not especially honest, tend not to make self-inculpatory statements unless they believe them to be true. This assumption does not extend to assertions that are not self-inculpatory.

**Concurrence** (Scalia, J.). A statement can be inculpatory without containing a confession. Additionally, a statement is not inadmissible merely because it implicates another person, although naming another has bearing on whether the statement fits the exception. The relevant inquiry is whether the particular remark meets the standard set forth by the Rule.

**Concurrence** (Ginsberg, Blackmun, Stevens, and Souter, JJ.). A statement implicating another is inadmissible under the Confrontation Clause; an arrested person always has a strong incentive to shift the blame. The case should be remanded only to determine whether the admission of Harris's statements was harmless error.

**Concurrence** (Kennedy, Thomas, JJ., Rehnquist, C.J.). The Court's interpretation of Rule 804(b)(3), which allows no statements collateral to a statement against interest, renders the "against penal interest" provision of the Rule meaningless. When determining whether a statement against penal interest that inculpates the accused is admissible, the court should first determine whether the declarant's statement contained a fact against his penal interest. If so, the court should admit all statements related to the statement against penal interest subject to two limitations: First, the court should exclude collateral statements rendered unreliable due to their self-serving nature (*e.g.*, statements shifting the blame to another person). Second, inculpatory statements made with a self-serving motivation should be excluded (*e.g.*, statements made to gain favorable treatment from the prosecution).

**Comment.** The *Williamson* Court left open the question of whether the against-interest exception is "firmly-rooted" for purposes of the Confrontation Clause when applied to a confession implicating the accused. Subsequently, the Court determined that if the exception is not firmly rooted, such statements may be admitted only if specific factors indicate that it is trustworthy. [Lilly v. Virginia, 527 U.S. 116 (1999)] The Court further clarified this concept as applied to specific situations in *Crawford v. Washington*, 541 U.S. 36 (2004), where it declared that, at the very least, courts cannot admit statements given to police by alleged co-offenders directly implicating the accused. Therefore, after *Crawford*, the statements in *Williamson* and *Lilly* would not be admissible.

---

5.  **Statement of Personal or Family History.** Rule 804(b)(4) defines the exception for a statement against interest as follows:

    (A)  A statement concerning the declarant's own birth, adoption, marriage, divorce, legitimacy, relationship by blood, adoption, or marriage, ancestry, or other similar fact of personal or family history, even though declarant had no means of acquiring personal knowledge of the matter stated; or

    (B)  A statement concerning the foregoing matters, and death also, of another person, if the declarant was related to the other by blood, adoption, or marriage or was so intimately associated with the other's family as to be likely to have accurate information concerning the matter declared.

6.  **Forfeiture by Misconduct.** Under Rule 804(b)(6), statements against a party who wrongfully made the declarant unavailable to testify are admissible against that party.

---

## E.  THE CATCHALL EXCEPTION

1.  **Introduction.** In 1997, Congress consolidated two previously identical provisions that describe a residual or catchall exception. The new rule, Rule 807, allows an exception to the hearsay rule for statements not specifically covered by Rule 803 or Rule 804 if it has equivalent circumstantial guarantees of trustworthiness, so long as the court determines that:

    a.  The statement is offered as evidence of a material fact;

    b.  The statement is more probative on the point for which it is offered than any other evidence which the proponent can procure through reasonable efforts; and

c.   The general purposes of these rules and the interests of justice will best be served by admission of the statement into evidence.

2.   **Procedural Requirement.** Rule 807 includes the following notice requirement:

> [A] statement may not be admitted under this exception unless the proponent of it makes known to the adverse party sufficiently in advance of the trial or hearing to provide the adverse party with a fair opportunity to prepare to meet it, the proponent's intention to offer the statement and the particulars of it, including the name and address of the declarant.

3.   **Proof of Exonerating Facts--**

---

## State v. Weaver, 554 N.W.2d 240 (Iowa 1996).

---

**Facts.** Weaver (D) picked up an 11-month-old girl from the girl's mother's house. An hour later, D called 911 because the girl had stopped breathing. The next day, the girl died. The autopsy disclosed several old and recent injuries that were consistent with shaken baby syndrome. Doctors testified that certain injuries were a week or two old, but the hemorrhage causing the respiratory arrest that killed the girl occurred shortly before she arrived at the hospital. D was charged with murder and child endangerment. After the first trial produced a hung jury, D was convicted of murder in a second trial before the judge alone. The judge declined to grant a new trial based on affidavits D obtained from witnesses who said the girl's mother, Tessia Mathes, told them that the girl had hit her head on a coffee table on the morning before D picked her up. The Iowa Supreme Court remanded for consideration of a second new trial motion based on additional affidavits from three other women who had heard Mathes make the statement. This time, the judge found the testimony had sufficient guarantees of trustworthiness to require a new trial. The Iowa Supreme Court granted review.

**Issue.** Where out-of-court statements do not fit within one of the enumerated hearsay exceptions, may a court admit them as evidence so long as they have equivalent guarantees of trustworthiness?

**Held.** Yes. Judgment affirmed.

♦   The three additional affidavits all asserted the following facts: the witnesses met at a specific restaurant every Wednesday; Mathes worked at the restaurant; and shortly after the girl died, Mathes told the witnesses that she had been dressing the girl when the girl hit her head on the coffee table. Two of the witnesses said Mathes told them that the baby was knocked unconscious.

♦   The court determined that this evidence was trustworthy and therefore admissible under the residual exception for the following reasons:

(i)   The witnesses are credible;

(ii)     The declarant, Mathes, is available to testify;

(iii)    The statement was made shortly after the incident;

(iv)     The declarant had firsthand knowledge of the substance of the statement;

(v)      The statement was unambiguous;

(vi)     The statement was in response to an open-ended question;

(vii)    The statement was made to multiple people who agree on its substance;

(viii)   A similar account was made on other occasions; and

(ix)     The statement is corroborated by objective medical evidence.

♦   D also produced an expert witness who testified that the respiratory arrest was caused when a previously existing subdural hematoma rebled, and that the coffee table incident caused the rebleeding. This shows that the evidence probably would have changed the result at trial, so the order for a new trial was appropriate.

**Comment.** In the third trial, D was acquitted on all charges.

---

## F.   THE CONSTITUTION AND HEARSAY

1.   **Introduction.** The Sixth Amendment of the Constitution provides that in all criminal prosecutions, the accused shall enjoy the right "to be confronted with the witnesses against him; to have compulsory process for obtaining witnesses in his favor, and to have the Assistance of Counsel for his defense." The use of hearsay appears to contradict this constitutional right. The courts have reconciled the right of confrontation with the practicalities of the courtroom by balancing the competing interests. Generally, the court allows the use of hearsay exceptions.

2.   **Modern Approach.** In *California v. Green*, 399 U.S. 149 (1970), the Court held that at least as a matter of constitutional law, there is no prohibition against using reported testimony when the witness is present at the trial. This is true even when the witness has a lapse of memory, claims a Fifth Amendment privilege, or simply refuses to testify. The rationale is that any claimed prejudice to the accused in not cross-examining the declarant at the time the statement was made is offset by the fact that the declarant can be cross-

examined at trial, and any inconsistency between his testimony in court and his statement made outside of court can be pointed out to the jury.

### a. Two-pronged approach--

## Ohio v. Roberts, 448 U.S. 56 (1980).

**Facts.** Roberts (D) was tried and convicted of forgery and possession of stolen credit cards, based in part on rebuttal to D's testimony. The rebuttal consisted of a transcript of the testimony of the victim's daughter at a preliminary hearing. D had called the witness at that hearing and examined her then. The prosecution was unable to locate the witness for D's trial. D claimed that admission of the transcript violated the Confrontation Clause. On appeal, D's conviction was overturned by the Ohio Supreme Court. The State appeals.

**Issue.** Does admission of hearsay evidence under one of the recognized exceptions violate the Confrontation Clause of the Constitution?

**Held.** No. Judgment reversed.

◆ If read literally, the Confrontation Clause would require that any statement made by an out-of-court declarant be excluded. This interpretation was not intended.

◆ The Confrontation Clause restricts the range of admissible hearsay in two ways:

(i) the prosecution must either produce the declarant whose statement is offered or demonstrate that the declarant is unavailable; and

(ii) hearsay may be admitted only when the declarant is unavailable and then only when the hearsay has the requisite degree of trustworthiness, which requires indicia of reliability.

◆ Reliability of hearsay may be inferred for Confrontation Clause purposes when it falls within a firmly rooted hearsay exception.

### b. Cross-examination required by Confrontation Clause--

## Crawford v. Washington, 541 U.S. 36 (2004).

**Facts.** Crawford (D) and his wife, Sylvia, confronted Lee at his apartment after Lee allegedly attempted to rape Sylvia. A fight ensued, and D stabbed Lee. D was charged with assault and attempted murder. At trial, D testified that he thought that Lee had reached for something in his pocket right before he began stabbing Lee and that the stabbing had been in self-defense. Sylvia had made a statement to police indicating that Lee's hands may have been open and empty at the time of the stabbing. Under Washington's marital privilege law, Sylvia did not testify at D's trial, but prosecutors introduced a recording of her statement to police in an effort to negate the self-defense claim. D objected to introduction of the statement, arguing that its admission violates the Confrontation Clause. Relying on *Ohio v. Roberts*, the trial court admitted the statement, finding that it met the reliability test, *i.e.*, that the witness was unavailable, and that the statement bore "particularized guarantees of trustworthiness." D was convicted. The court of appeals reversed, but the Washington Supreme Court upheld the conviction based on a finding that the statement bore guarantees of trustworthiness in that it "interlocked" with statements made by D. The United States Supreme Court granted certiorari.

**Issue.** In a criminal trial, may a prior statement from a witness who is not present at the trial be admitted into evidence against the accused when the accused had no opportunity to cross-examine the witness when the prior statement was given?

**Held.** No. Judgment reversed.

♦ *Roberts* held that an unavailable witness's out-of-court statement may be admitted so long as it has adequate indicia of reliability, defined as falling within a "firmly rooted hearsay exception" or having "particularized guarantees of trustworthiness." The Confrontation Clause itself guarantees the right to confrontation with the witnesses against an accused, but this could be interpreted to apply only to those witnesses who testify at trial instead of those whose statements are offered at trial.

♦ When the founders adopted the Confrontation Clause, they were concerned about issues that had arisen under common law. For example, Sir Walter Raleigh had been tried for treason, and the primary evidence against him was an out-of-court statement made by his alleged accomplice. The court refused to require this witness to appear in court, and Raleigh was convicted and sentenced to death. While this procedure complied with civil law, English law adopted a right of confrontation to avoid abuses.

♦ The Confrontation Clause was directed at aspects of the criminal procedure of the Civil Law System, especially the use of *ex parte* examinations as evidence against an accused. Accordingly, the right of confrontation is not limited to in-court testimony, but applies to any witness against the accused, which includes any "testimonial" statements. Interrogations by law enforcement officers, such as the one that produced Sylvia's statement in this case, fall within this class of statements.

♦ Despite the holding of *Roberts*, the outcome of prior cases remained faithful to the principle that testimonial statements of witnesses absent from trial are admissible only where the declarant is unavailable, and only where the accused has had a prior opportunity to cross-examine the declarant.

- Where testimonial statements are involved, the right of confrontation is not subject to the rules of evidence or a vague notion of "reliability." The Confrontation Clause provides a procedural guarantee, not a substantive one. It requires that reliability be assessed in a particular manner: cross-examination. Dispensing with confrontation because testimony is obviously reliable would be like dispensing with a jury trial because the defendant is obviously guilty.

- The *Roberts* holding does not comply with the Confrontation Clause because it would admit core testimonial statements that the Confrontation Clause is intended to exclude. This case demonstrates how *Roberts* is both unpredictable and inconsistent; the trial court, the appellate court, and the state supreme court all reached different conclusions about the reliability of Sylvia's out-of-court statement. Courts cannot substitute their own measures of reliability for the one mandated by the Confrontation Clause.

**Comment.** The Court noted that non-testimonial hearsay is governed by state hearsay law, while testimonial evidence is covered by the Confrontation Clause and cannot be admitted without a showing of unavailability and a prior opportunity for cross-examination. The scope of "testimonial" evidence is not clearly spelled out, but it does cover prior testimony at a preliminary hearing, before a grand jury, or at a former trial, and it also applies to police interrogations.

---

3.   **"New Hearsay"--**

---

**Idaho v. Wright**, 497 U.S. 805 (1990).

---

**Facts.** Wright (D) was charged with aiding Giles in sexually abusing D's two daughters, ages five and a half and two and a half. One of the girls told an adult about the abuse. Medical exams showed they had been abused. A pediatrician, Dr. Jambura, interviewed the younger daughter, who told him that Giles had sexual contact with her, but did it a lot more with her sister. At D's trial, the court admitted Dr. Jambura's testimony under the equivalent of Federal Rule 803(24), the general exception to the hearsay rule, on the ground that the child witness was unavailable and the evidence was sufficiently reliable. Consequently, D was convicted. The Idaho Supreme Court reversed on the ground that admitting the statement violated the Confrontation Clause of the Constitution. The Supreme Court granted certiorari.

**Issue.** Where a victim is too young to testify, may the prosecution use testimony regarding the young victim's statements to an examining physician?

**Held.** No. Judgment affirmed.

- The Confrontation Clause restricts the range of admissible hearsay by requiring that (i) the declarant must be present, or her unavailability must be demonstrated; and (ii) if the witness is unavailable, her statement is admissible only if it bears adequate indicia of reliability. Reliability is inferred when the evidence satisfies a "firmly rooted" hearsay exception or when there is a showing of particularized guarantees of trustworthiness.

♦ Idaho's residual hearsay exception is not a firmly rooted hearsay exception for Confrontation Clause purposes. Therefore, the State had to show "particularized guarantees of trustworthiness" showing the challenged statement to be so trustworthy that cross-examination would add little to its reliability.

♦ The statement offered must pass this test by virtue of its inherent trustworthiness, considering the totality of the circumstances. However, corroborating evidence may not be considered in assessing the trustworthiness of a hearsay statement.

♦ The State did not make the required showing of "particularized guarantees of trustworthiness." The totality of the circumstances in which the victim responded to the doctor's questions does not provide a special reason to suppose that the incriminating statements were particularly trustworthy. Additionally, these circumstances of reliability were not comparable to traditional hearsay exceptions such as excited utterances or statements given for medical diagnosis or treatment.

**Comment.** This case applies the *Roberts* doctrine, which has been changed by *Crawford*. Many states have adopted statutes that allow the use of statements by children regarding sexual abuse. Such statements made to prosecutors or other officials who work with the prosecutors would be considered testimonial under *Crawford*. This suggests that the statements would not be admissible unless the child also testifies at trial, where she could be subjected to cross-examination.

———————

# V. ADDITIONAL RELEVANCE ISSUES

## A. CHARACTER

1. **Character as Evidence of Conduct.** Character evidence is evidence of particular human traits such as honesty, violence, etc. It is normally used to show a person's disposition to act in a particular way and is thus often referred to as "propensity" evidence.

   a. **Methods of proving character.** There are three basic types of evidence of a person's character. Under Federal Rule 405(b), all three may be used to prove character when character is an ultimate issue in the case.

      1) **Personal opinion.** One or more persons may offer their personal opinion (based on observation) as to some person's character for honesty or some other trait.

      2) **Reputation.** Testimony as to a person's "general reputation" in the community may be given, whether the witness actually knows the person in question or not.

      3) **Specific acts.** Evidence may be given of specific acts that a person has done that would lead to inferences as to his character.

2. **Character to Prove Conduct on a Particular Occasion.**

   a. **Introduction.** In some cases, character itself is not in issue, but character evidence may still be used as circumstantial evidence from which an inference can be drawn as to the existence or nonexistence of some fact that is in issue; *e.g.,* if the issue is whether A shot B, character evidence that A has a violent temper is circumstantial evidence supporting an inference that A did the shooting. Because the probative value of such evidence is slight, however, and its potential for unfair prejudice is great, this use of character evidence is restricted.

   b. **Civil cases.** In civil cases, character evidence will not normally be admitted to prove that the person whose character is sought to be shown engaged in certain conduct (or did so with certain intent). [Fed. R. Evid. 404(a)] For example, in a negligence case, evidence that the defendant had a reputation for careless driving would not be admissible. Although relevant, courts feel that this kind of evidence is too prejudicial, time consuming, etc. However, a growing number of courts are permitting reputation evidence in civil cases when a person is charged with an act (such as fraud) involving "moral turpitude." The reason is that a judgment against the defendant could be as serious as a criminal conviction.

**c.    Criminal cases.**

**1)    Defendant's evidence of good character.** A defendant is always allowed to introduce evidence of his good character to show the improbability that he committed the crime charged. [Fed. R. Evid. 404(a)(1)] This is a matter of leniency, and applies whether or not the defendant testifies. Most courts require that the evidence be relevant to the crime charged, but some allow general proof of good character.

**a)    Reputation.** Traditionally, only the defendant's reputation in the community at the time of the crime charged could be used as evidence of good character. Opinion testimony and specific act evidence were inadmissible.

**b)    Opinion.** The modern trend and Federal Rule 405(a) allow evidence of opinion as well as reputation evidence. However, specific act evidence still is not admissible because it is not probative and distracts from the real issues.

**2)    Rebuttal of good character evidence.**

**a)    Basic rules.** The prosecution normally cannot introduce evidence of the defendant's bad character, but it can rebut reputation or opinion evidence produced by the defendant. The most frequent rebuttal evidence arises from cross-examination of the defendant's character witnesses. To test their credibility, the prosecution is allowed to ask the witnesses about the defendant's prior specific acts. This can include arrests or indictments, as these test the witness's knowledge of the defendant's reputation or the basis for the witness's opinion. If the witness denies knowing of the prior acts, most jurisdictions do not allow independent evidence of such acts.

**3.    Specific Acts of Misconduct Admissible If Independently Relevant.**

**a.    Introduction.** Evidence of other crimes or misconduct is generally excluded because it could lead a jury to convict on the ground of the defendant's criminal disposition instead of his guilt. However, specific act evidence may be admitted under Federal Rule 404(b) if the evidence: (i) is relevant to an issue other than the defendant's character (*e.g.*, to show motive, inent, or identity); (ii) possesses probative value that is not substantially outweighed by its undue prejudice; and (iii) meets the other requirements of Federal Rule 403.

## b.   Examples.

1) **Motive, intent, knowledge, or state of mind.** Specific acts may be admitted to show that the defendant did the act for which he is being tried with guilty knowledge or intent. For example, if the defendant is being tried for a crime that requires that he act "knowingly," evidence that he had earlier been convicted of the same crime would prove such knowledge. It also may be used to show that he had the motive to do the act with which he is charged.

2) **Scheme, plan, or conspiracy.** Evidence of other criminal acts may be admitted to show the existence of a larger scheme, plan, or conspiracy of which the present crime is merely one part.

3) **Identity.** The identity exception of Rule 404(b) has a limited scope. It does not allow admission of extrinsic acts that are merely similar, but only those that have such a high degree of similarity as to mark the specific offense as the handiwork of the accused; *i.e.*, the modus operandi method of proving identity.

4) **Pattern.** The term "pattern" refers to a series of acts that collectively identify the offender. It is used to show identity or sometimes membership in a conspiracy. Therefore, the temporal proximity of the acts is important. Over a long period of time, other people will commit similar crimes, diminishing the value of the evidence to show identity. The existence of a pattern alone does not suffice to permit introduction of evidence of the pattern. The pattern must show identity, intent, plan, absence of mistake, etc., to make the evidence admissible.

5) **Other.** Similar acts or related misconduct may be used to prove any *relevant* fact other than the accused's general bad character or criminal disposition.

4.   **Prior Sexual Conduct.** To protect the privacy of victims and encourage reporting of sexual crimes, most states have adopted rules against inquiry into the prior sexual conduct of victims. The rape shield statutes avoid prejudice to the victim, jury confusion, and waste of time on collateral matters. However, such evidence cannot be excluded in violation of the defendant's Confrontation Clause rights. This means that evidence of a victim's having previously made false charges would normally be admissible, as would cross-examination aimed at exposing the witness's motivation to testify.

## B.  SIMILAR HAPPENINGS

1.   **Other Contracts.** When the same parties are involved in other contractual transactions, evidence of such other contracts will be received if relevant to

show the probable meaning that the parties gave to the contract presently in dispute. Courts seldom, however, admit a party's contracts with third persons for this same purpose.

2.  **Previous Accidents and Injuries.**

    a.  **Prior accidents.** Prior accidents to others resulting from a condition or activity conducted by the defendant may be shown to prove the defendant's negligence in the present case. Such evidence may be used to prove that the defendant had knowledge of the danger involved or that a reasonable person would have. It also may show that the injury was in fact caused by the defective condition or situation. To have the evidence admitted, the proponent must show:

        1)  Substantial similarity of existing conditions, and

        2)  Close proximity in time between the two accidents.

    b.  **Proof of subsequent accidents.** Courts do not permit a party to show subsequent accidents to prove that a condition or product for which the defendant is responsible caused an earlier injury to the plaintiff or that the defendant had knowledge of the dangerous condition. However, courts will permit such proof if it is used as circumstantial evidence that a dangerous condition existed at the time of the accident being litigated.

    c.  **Absence of other accidents.** Traditionally, courts did not admit evidence that there were no similar accidents or occurrences in order to show that the defendant did not have knowledge of the danger or that the condition defendant is allegedly responsible for did not cause the harm or injury. The modern trend allows this evidence in some circumstances.

## C.  SUBSEQUENT REPAIRS OR PRECAUTIONS

1.  **Introduction.** A plaintiff may desire to introduce evidence that following his injury, the defendant made some repair or modification to her premises or an instrumentality alleged to be defective and the cause of the injuries. Such evidence generally is held not admissible to prove negligence or other culpable conduct in connection with the event. However, subsequent repairs are admissible to impeach the defendant's witnesses, to show ownership or control of the premises, to show that the defendant was trying to conceal or destroy evidence, or to show that precautionary measures were feasible. The evidence must relate to a real issue in the case; if the feasibility of precautionary measures is not in dispute, evidence of subsequent repairs would not be allowed if proof of feasibility was the only asserted basis for admission.

## 2. Subsequent Change in Medical Protocol--

---

**Tuer v. McDonald,** 701 A.2d 1101 (Md. 1997).

---

**Facts.** Tuer (P) sued McDonald (D), a cardiac surgeon, and D's partner for medical malpractice arising from the death of her husband after cardiac surgery. P's husband had been given Heparin a few days prior to surgery, but this was discontinued the morning of the scheduled surgery to avoid his having the anticoagulant in his blood during surgery. The operation was postponed until later in the day, and in the meantime, P's husband went into cardiac arrest. He was resuscitated and underwent surgery. He died the day after surgery. As a result, the hospital changed the protocol with respect to discontinuing Heparin for patients with stable angina. At the trial, D moved to exclude any reference to the change in practice. The court ruled that the evidence would be admissible to show that restarting the Heparin was "feasible" if D denied the feasibility of doing so. During his testimony, D stated that it would have been unsafe to restart the Heparin after postponing the surgery. P sought to introduce the change in protocol to rebut D's statement, but the court disallowed it because D stated that Heparin is sometimes used later in surgery. The jury found for D. P appeals.

**Issue.** May evidence of a change in medical protocol be admitted to rebut a physician's statement that the new protocol would have been unsafe at the time he made the decision to follow the protocol that was in effect at the time?

**Held.** No. Judgment affirmed.

♦　There are two justifications for excluding evidence of subsequent remedial measures to prove culpability. The first is that the subsequent conduct is not actually an admission, and the second is that public policy encourages people to take remedial measures.

♦　P claims that the evidence should have been admitted to show the feasibility of taking patients into surgery with Heparin in their blood. The feasibility exception can be construed narrowly so that it applies only when the defendant claims the measures were not physically, technologically, or economically possible. Some courts apply a broader notion of feasibility, including that which is capable of being utilized successfully and not that which is merely possible. In this case, D's statement does not reflect a statement that restarting Heparin was not feasible, but instead that it was not advisable after balancing the risks of the alternatives. Therefore, the statement does not fall within the feasibility exception.

♦　The impeachment exception is interpreted narrowly by the courts and is not normally admissible if offered for simple contradiction of a defense witness's testimony. Applying this standard, the subsequent change in protocol would not impeach D's statement about the decision he made based on his knowledge and experience at the time. The fact that the protocol changed later does not suggest that D did not honestly believe that his decision was appropriate at the time.

♦ The only reasonable inference from D's testimony was that he and his colleagues reevaluated the relative risks after what happened in this case and decided the new protocol was safer. This type of reevaluation is what the exclusionary rule is intended to encourage.

----

## D. SETTLEMENT AND COMPROMISE

1. **Civil Cases.** To encourage parties to settle their disputes out of court, courts will not permit a party to offer in evidence the fact that the adverse party made an offer to compromise or settle the claim that is the subject of the action. Statements made in connection with such settlement offers also are inadmissible.

2. **Guilty Pleas.** If the defendant entered a guilty plea in a criminal case, it may be introduced in a subsequent civil trial. However, the defendant may explain the circumstances surrounding the guilty plea. If the guilty plea was not accepted by the court, it may not be admitted in a subsequent trial.

# VI. COMPETENCY OF WITNESSES

## A. INTRODUCTION

1. **Basic Principles.** "Competency" refers to the admissibility of a witness's testimony. While the *weight* to be given to a witness's testimony is up to the trier of fact (jury or judge in nonjury trials), a witness's competency to testify is a question of law to be decided by the trial judge.

2. **Common Law.** At common law, there were a number of grounds upon which a person could be disqualified from giving testimony; *e.g.,* having a financial interest in the outcome of the suit (the parties); being married to a party; lack of religious belief; conviction of a felony; race; infancy; and mental derangement.

## B. MODERN APPROACH

1. **Adaptation of Common Law.** Although certain common law grounds have been repudiated entirely (*e.g.,* race, lack of religious belief, and felony conviction), many states retain the common law grounds to some extent.

   a. **Some states abolish.** In some states, however, all grounds upon which a witness was disqualified from testifying at common law have been abolished. Certain factors (*e.g.,* financial interest, felony conviction, etc.) may go to the weight of a witness's testimony, but they do not affect its admissibility. [*See, e.g.*, Cal. Evid. Code §700]

   b. **Federal Rules—*Erie* doctrine.** The Federal Rules adopt the trend toward abolition of all grounds for disqualification, except when the case turns on state law (*e.g.,* diversity jurisdiction cases), in which case the competency of a witness must be determined in accordance with the state law. [Fed. R. Evid. 601]

2. **Requirements in General.** To be competent to testify, a witness must meet the following requirements. [Cal. Evid. Code §§701, 702]

   a. **Ability to communicate.** The witness must be capable of expressing herself so as to be understood by the jury—either directly or through an interpreter. If the witness testifies through an interpreter, it must be shown that the interpreter is qualified in the foreign language in question and is under oath to make a true translation. [Fed. R. Evid. 604]

   b. **Obligation of truthfulness.** The witness must be capable of understanding the obligation to tell the truth.

c. **Personal knowledge.** The witness must have personal knowledge and recollection regarding the matter upon which she is called to testify.

    1) **Federal Rules.** Note that under the Federal Rules, personal knowledge is the *only* requirement. The witness's ability to express herself and her understanding of the obligation to tell the truth affect only the weight of her testimony, not its admissibility. [Fed. R. Evid. 602, 601 note]

d. **Time of competency.** The above requirements refer to the condition of the witness at the time she is called to testify. Thus, the fact that a witness's recollection had vanished after the event in question but was restored prior to trial (*e.g.*, by a writing, hypnosis, etc.), does not render her incompetent as a witness.

3. **Satisfaction of Minimum Requirements--**

## United States v. Lightly, 677 F.2d 1027 (4th Cir. 1982).

**Facts.** McKinley, an inmate, was seriously wounded during an assault in his cell. Two fellow inmates, McDuffie and Lightly (D), were implicated. A court-appointed psychiatrist found McDuffie incompetent to stand trial and criminally insane at the time of the assault. Only D was indicted. At trial, McKinley and three other inmates testified that McKinley was attacked by D and McDuffie. D and three other inmates testified that D witnessed the fight between McKinley and McDuffie and entered the cell to stop the fight. D sought to have McDuffie testify that McDuffie alone attacked McKinley. The court ruled McDuffie incompetent to testify because he was criminally insane and incompetent to stand trial. D was convicted of assault with intent to commit murder. D appeals.

**Issue.** Is a witness incompetent to testify if he is criminally insane and incompetent to stand trial?

**Held.** No. Judgment reversed and case remanded.

♦ Every witness is presumed competent to testify unless he does not have personal knowledge of the matter or the capacity to recall, or does not understand the duty to testify truthfully. A person's insanity, by itself, does not render him incompetent to testify.

♦ McDuffie's physician testified that he had a sufficient memory, he understood the oath, and he could communicate what he saw. This is all that is required. Because his testimony would have corroborated D's version of the events, his disqualification as a witness was not harmless error.

# C. OATH REQUIREMENT

1. **Introduction.** All witnesses are required to swear an oath or make an affirmation that they will tell the truth. The oath or affirmation is intended to assure that the witness will tell the truth, but it also subjects the witness to prosecution for perjury if she lies.

2. **Defendant's Own Testimony--**

---

## United States v. Fowler, 605 F.2d 181 (5th Cir. 1979).

---

**Facts.** Fowler (D), a tax protestor who had not filed tax returns for many years, was charged with willful failure to file returns for the years 1971-75. D conducted his own defense at trial. He sought to testify despite refusing to either swear or affirm that he would tell the truth or submit to cross-examination. He refused to even make the statement, "I state that I will tell the truth in my testimony." The court declined to allow D to testify. D was convicted. D appeals.

**Issue.** May a criminal defendant testify on his own behalf if he refuses to swear or affirm that he will tell the truth?

**Held.** No. Judgment affirmed.

♦ No witness has the right to testify except on penalty of perjury and subject to cross-examination. A claim otherwise is frivolous.

---

# D. CHILDREN AS WITNESSES

1. **Basic Rule.** A child of any age may be permitted to testify if the trial judge is satisfied that the child possesses the ability to observe, recollect, and communicate. Some state statutes raise a presumption that children over a certain age (*e.g.,* 10 years) are competent, while the competency of younger children must be determined by the trial court.

2. **Six-Year-Old Witness--**

---

## Ricketts v. Delaware, 488 A.2d 856 (Del. 1985).

---

**Facts.** Ricketts (D) was charged with first degree rape of his girlfriend's five-year-old daughter. At trial, the victim, who was by then six years old, was called to testify. D objected. The court conducted a voir dire examination during which the girl said she knew a lie was a thing that is not true, and that it was a bad thing to tell a lie. She also promised to tell the truth. She did not understand the concept of perjury, however. The court deemed her competent to testify. Using anatomically correct dolls and drawings, the girl testified that D had anally raped her. D was convicted. D appeals, claiming the child should not have been allowed to testify.

**Issue.** May a six-year-old victim testify in court if she does not understand the concept of perjury?

**Held.** Yes. Judgment affirmed.

♦ Under Delaware Rule of Evidence 601, every person is presumed competent to testify except as otherwise provided in the rules. So long as the judge was satisfied that the victim in this case understood her obligation to tell the truth and the difference between truth and falsehood, he properly allowed her to testify.

♦ D claims that the voir dire examination showed that the girl did not understand the oath. However, her promise to tell the truth is a sufficient affirmation that she would testify truthfully.

---

## E. HYPNOSIS

1. **Introduction.** The use of hypnosis presents special problems because of its potential to alter memory. Although hypnosis may be a useful investigatory technique, it is subject to significant problems:

   a. The hypnotized person is highly subject to the hypnotist's suggestions;

   b. The hypnotized subject has a strong desire to please the hypnotist and may fantasize or confuse thoughts that become part of her recall to please the hypnotist;

   c. Once hypnotized, the person becomes absolutely confident in the matters "recalled" during the trance; and

   d. During the hypnotic trance, neither the hypnotist nor the subject can distinguish between true and pseudo memories. This inability to distinguish memories continues past the hypnotic state so that it becomes impossible to tell what memories are true even when the subject is fully awake and testifying at trial under oath.

2. **Judicial Approaches.** There are three approaches taken by the courts with respect to hypnotized witnesses.

   a. Some courts hold that recall aided by hypnosis is admissible, and that the problems mentioned above merely affect the weight of the testimony.

b.  Other courts completely exclude any recall that has been affected by hypnosis.

c.  Some courts allow hypnotic recall if certain safeguards are followed, including having the subject record a complete, detailed description of the facts remembered prior to the session and accurately recording the entire session. In some jurisdictions, the subject is allowed to testify only regarding facts demonstrably recalled prior to hypnosis.

3.  **Substantive Considerations.**

   a.  **Type of memory loss.** The type of memory loss that the hypnosis is intended to overcome is a critical factor. When there is a pathological reason for the loss, such as a traumatic neurosis, hypnosis is likely to result in reliable memory. When the "loss" is due to a lack of recollection or some discernible motivation, the hypnotic memory is likely to be fanciful or otherwise unreliable.

   b.  **Hypnotic susceptibility.** Some subjects are more amenable to hypnosis than others, and this may affect the reliability of the results.

4.  **Procedural Requirements.** When testimony from hypnotized witnesses is allowed, the following safeguards are typically required.

   a.  **Professional hypnotist.** The person conducting the hypnotic session must be a professional able to testify about the substantive considerations set out *supra*.

   b.  **Independence.** The professional must be unbiased and not regularly employed by any interested party.

   c.  **Disclosure of information provided.** All information given to the hypnotist by an interested party must be appropriately recorded to allow review in cases of alleged suggestion to the subject.

   d.  **Pre-session account.** Before entering a hypnotic state, the subject should make a full, detailed description of the facts remembered to that point.

   e.  **All contacts recorded.** All contacts between the hypnotist and the subject must be recorded to allow review.

   f.  **One-on-one session.** The hypnotic session must not be attended by anyone other than the hypnotist and the subject.

5.  **Hypnotically Refreshed Testimony--**

---

**Rock v. Arkansas**, 483 U.S. 44 (1987).

---

**Facts.** Rock (D) and her husband Frank had a fight one night after he refused to let D eat some pizza and would not allow her to leave their apartment to get something else to eat. Police responded and found Frank on the floor with a bullet wound in his chest. D was upset, told the police not to let Frank die, and stated that Frank had choked her and thrown her against the wall before she picked up a gun and shot him. D could not remember the precise details of the shooting, however, and at her attorney's suggestion, she submitted to hypnosis. Although she did not relate any new information during the hypnosis sessions, she later remembered that she had her thumb on the hammer of the gun but did not have her finger on the trigger. She also remembered that the gun discharged when Frank grabbed her arm during a scuffle. An inspection of the gun showed that it was defective and could be fired if hit or dropped without anyone pulling the trigger. D was charged with manslaughter. The prosecutor moved to exclude D's testimony. The trial court ruled that no hypnotically refreshed testimony would be admitted and limited D's testimony to matters she related before being hypnotized. D was convicted. The state supreme court upheld the conviction, holding that the dangers of admitting hypnotically refreshed testimony outweigh any probative value it may have. Any prejudice to D resulted from her own actions in seeking the hypnosis. The Supreme Court granted certiorari.

**Issue.** May an accused testify even if her testimony was hypnotically refreshed?

**Held.** Yes. Judgment vacated and case remanded.

♦ D clearly has a constitutional right to testify in her own defense. In light of the constitutional right involved, a state may not prevent an accused from presenting material witnesses, nor may it arbitrarily exclude material portions of a witness's testimony through application of rules of evidence. This does not prevent limitation on the right to present relevant testimony, but restrictions may not be arbitrary or disproportionate to the purposes they are designed to serve.

♦ Arkansas applies a per se rule to prohibit admission of hypnotically refreshed testimony. This rule is detrimental to any defendant who submits to hypnosis regardless of the circumstances. In this case, it prevented D from describing events that were corroborated by other witnesses and undermined the significance of the gun inspection.

♦ The use of hypnosis, especially in criminal cases, is controversial. It has been used to obtain evidence that was later confirmed by independent evidence, but it also introduces a possibility of inaccuracy in three ways: (i) the subject may try to please the hypnotist with imagined answers; (ii) the subject may confabulate or provide details from the imagination; and (iii) the subject's memory hardens, giving him greater confidence in the memory, whether correct or false.

♦ The risk of inaccuracies associated with the use of hypotically refreshed testimony may he minimized by using procedural safeguards such as requiring the use of independent and trained hypnotists and recording hypnotic sessions. More

traditional means also may be used to verify the accuracy of hypnotically refreshed testimony, *e.g.*, independent evidence may be presented to corroborate
hypotically refreshed testimony and cross-examination may be used to reveal
inconsistencies. Futhermore, the jury can be educated about the risks of hypnosis through expert testimony and cautionary instructions from the judge.

◆ Although a state has a legitimate interest in barring unreliable evidence, that
interest does not permit per se exclusions of evidence that may be reliable in an
individual case. Hypnotically refreshed testimony is sufficiently trustworthy to
be evaluated on a case-by-case basis. In this case, D's testimony was corroborated by the gun's defective condition and recordings of the hypnotic sessions
indicate that responses were not suggested to D.

---

## F. COMPETENCY AS AFFECTED BY CONNECTION WITH THE TRIBUNAL

1. **Jurors as Witnesses.**

   a. **Traditional rule.** The traditional and prevailing rule is that a juror is
   competent to testify in the case in which she is serving. (Of course,
   instances in which a juror will be called as an ordinary witness are rare,
   because voir dire generally will reveal that a juror has knowledge of the
   facts or parties.)

   b. **Modern rule.** However, the modern rule is that a juror may not testify
   (or give an affidavit) if either party objects. [Fed. R. Evid. 606; Cal.
   Evid. Code §704] Under this view, the opposing party must be afforded
   the opportunity to object to such testimony outside of the presence of
   the jury to avoid jury prejudice. [Fed. R. Evid. 606(a)]

   c. **Testimony as to jury deliberations.** There is a wide split of authority
   as to the extent to which jurors are permitted to testify in post-verdict
   proceedings for the purpose of attacking or supporting the jury verdict.

   1) The traditional view was that the jurors were incompetent to testify at all; *i.e.,* a juror was never allowed to "impeach her own
   verdict."

   2) Under the Federal Rules, juror testimony (or affidavits) is admissible only to show any outside influence improperly brought to
   bear on any member of the jury (*e.g.,* threats to the juror's family)
   or "extraneous prejudicial information improperly brought to the
   jury's attention" (*e.g.,* news releases). [Fed. R. Evid. 606(b)]

3) A few states go much further and permit jurors to testify as to "any fact or event" that occurred, inside or outside the jury room, that improperly influenced their verdict; *e.g.,* drunkenness, chance verdicts, etc. [*See, e.g.,* Cal. Evid. Code §1150]

### d.   Juror misconduct--

---

## Tanner v. United States, 483 U.S. 107 (1987).

---

**Facts.** Tanner and Conover (Ds) were convicted of federal mail fraud offenses. Before sentencing, Ds' attorney received a phone call from one of the jurors who related that several jurors had been drinking alcohol during the trial and slept through the afternoons. Ds moved for continuance of the sentencing date to permit interviews of jurors, an evidentiary hearing, and a new trial. The court continued the sentencing date and heard argument on the motion to interview jurors. After argument, the court held that jury testimony on intoxication could not be admitted to impeach the verdict under Federal Rule 606(b). The court denied the United States's (P's) motions to interview jurors and for a new trial. Ds appealed. While the appeal was pending, Ds' attorney was contacted by another juror who related that several jurors were drinking and using marijuana and cocaine during the trial. Ds filed another motion for a new trial based on this evidence. The court denied this motion as well. The court of appeals affirmed. The Supreme Court granted certiorari.

**Issue.** May a convicted defendant challenge a verdict based on juror misconduct using juror testimony about jurors' use of drugs and alcohol during the trial?

**Held.** No. Judgment affirmed.

♦   The common law rule held inadmissible any juror testimony offered to impeach a jury verdict. There were exceptions, but only when an "extraneous influence" allegedly affected the jury, such as a bailiff's comments.

♦   The distinction between external influences and internal influences has been generally followed. The distinction is not based on the location of the interference, but its nature. Allegations that a juror is physically or mentally incompetent are considered "internal" rather than "external."

♦   The rationale of this restricted use of juror testimony is to reinforce the independence and confidentiality of jury deliberations. The exception for external influences assists this insulating objective. An exception for internal influences might invalidate some verdicts based on improper juror behavior, but it would introduce juror harassment by losing parties and undermine the finality of judgments.

♦   Rule 606(b) reflects the common law rule. The legislative history of Rule 606(b) demonstrates that Congress specifically rejected a version of Rule 606(b) that would have allowed jurors to testify on juror conduct during deliberations, including intoxication. The legislative history also provides strong support that juror intoxication is not an extraneous influence.

♦ A juror's use of drugs and alcohol is an internal influence, just as is a lack of sleep, hunger, and illness. It is not an external influence. Therefore, it may not be admitted to invalidate a verdict.

---

2. **Judge as Witness.** A judge is not disqualified as a witness merely by virtue of the office. He may be subpoenaed or appear voluntarily to testify just as any other person. However, under the Federal Rules, the judge may not take the witness stand in the very case over which he is presiding. [Fed. R. Evid. 605]

# VII. DIRECT AND CROSS-EXAMINATION

## A.  DIRECT EXAMINATION

1.   **Introduction.** On direct examination of a witness, the lawyer generally may not ask leading questions. [Fed. R. Evid. 611(c)] The rule recognizes two exceptions:

   a.   **Necessary to develop testimony.** Leading questions may be used on direct examination if they are necessary to develop the witness's testimony (*e.g.*, when the witness experiences a loss of memory or is young, timid or confused, or physically infirm). The rule also allows the use of leading questions to elicit preliminary matters to save time.

   b.   **Hostile witness.** A party may interrogate a hostile witness with leading questions. Hostile witnesses include adverse parties, witnesses identified with an adverse party, and uncooperative witnesses.

2.   **Leading Questions Allowed--**

## Baker v. State, 371 A.2d 699 (Md. 1977).

**Facts.** Baker (D) was convicted of first degree murder and robbery, primarily on the statements of the murder victim related to the jury via a police officer. The officer said that the victim pointed out D as one of three women he had picked up at a bar. The victim left the bar with the three women and drove them to their stated destination. When they arrived at the destination, a man pulled the victim from his car, and the three women then kicked and beat him and stole his money. D had been detained by another police officer, and the testifying officer took the victim to where the other officer was holding D. At trial, D sought to have the testifying officer read a written report of the other officer that said that the victim told the officers that D was not one of the three women. The purpose of having the officer look at the report was not to identify it and introduce it into evidence, but was to stir an independent memory in the testifying officer about the events of the evening. The trial judge ruled that the officer could not be shown the report. D was convicted and appeals.

**Issue.** Was it error for the trial judge to refuse to permit a criminal defendant to attempt to refresh the recollection of a principal witness on cross-examination by showing the witness a report written by a fellow officer of the events described on direct examination?

**Held.** Yes. Judgment reversed and case remanded.

- Counsel may use different devices to revitalize the dimmed memory of a witness, including documents not otherwise admissible. This includes the use of an admittedly hearsay report of another police officer on the scene.

- The use of the hearsay writing is for purposes of refreshing memory. It is not the document that is going into evidence, but the recollection of the witness. The witness states his newly found memory, and it is his present recollection that he asserts as true, not the contents of the document. Refusing such an attempt to refresh recollection in a hostile witness on cross-examination resulted in prejudicial error.

**Comment.** Of course, present recollection refreshed is different than seeking to introduce a record of past recollection under the past recollection recorded exception to the hearsay rule. [Fed. R. Evid. 803(5)] Introducing a document under the hearsay exception (as opposed to a witness's refreshed testimony) requires that the witness made the record (or adopted it) at a time when the witness remembered the event, and that the witness can presently vouch for the fact that he knew the record was accurate when he made it. This substitutes for actual testimony if the witness cannot presently remember from independent recollection (even after attempts are made to refresh that memory).

---

## B. CROSS-EXAMINATION

1. **Introduction.** Ordinarily, leading questions are permitted on cross-examination. [Fed. R. Evid. 611(c)] Cross-examination should be limited to the subject matter of the direct examination and matters affecting the credibility of the witness. [Fed. R. Evid. 611(b)] Sometimes, cross-examination explores the preparation of the witness prior to trial, which can delve into what might be attorney work product.

2. **Cross-Examination with Privileged Material--**

---

**James Julian, Inc. v. Raytheon Co.**, 93 F.R.D. 138 (D. Del. 1982).

---

**Facts.** James Julian, Inc. (P) sued Raytheon Co. (D) and several labor organizations and union officers under the Sherman Act and National Labor Relations Act. While preparing witnesses for depositions, P's counsel assembled a binder that P's owners, officers, and employees reviewed prior to being deposed. During discovery, D sought production of the binder. P did not object to releasing the documents, but did object to releasing the binder itself on the ground that the selection and arrangement of the documents constituted privileged work product of P's lawyer. D argued that if the binder at one time was privileged, the privilege was waived when the binder was used to prepare witnesses. D moves to compel discovery.

**Issue.** Does Rule 612(2) apply to documents used to refresh a witness's memory before testifying when the documents are subject to a claim of privilege?

**Held.** Yes. Motion granted.

♦ The binder originally did reflect P's counsel's understanding of the case and was privileged work product. D claims that the privilege was waived under Rule 612 because it was used for witness preparation. Rule 612(2) changed the traditional rule that the use of a privileged document to refresh a witness's memory resulted in waiver only if it was used at the time of testimony.

♦ The legislative history of Rule 612 is unclear, but it does suggest that Congress intended the courts to balance the interests of full disclosure against the maintenance of confidentiality on a case-by-case basis. The courts that have addressed the issue generally agree that the use of protected documents to refresh a witness's memory prior to testifying constitutes a waiver of the protection.

♦ To allow lawyers to prepare witnesses with privileged documents would impose an unfair disadvantage on the cross-examiner who would have no access to the witness preparation documents.

♦ Without reviewing the binders, D's counsel cannot determine to what extent the witnesses' testimony has been affected by P's lawyer's presentation of the facts. To fairly balance the competing interests, D is entitled to know the content of the binders.

---

## C. EXCLUDING WITNESSES

1. **Introduction.** A party may request to have witnesses excluded from the courtroom so that they cannot hear the testimony of other witnesses. The judge normally honors this request, and may even make such an order without a request from a party. [Fed. R. Evid. 615] However, this rule does not authorize the exclusion of:

   a. A party who is a natural person;

   b. An officer or employee of a party which is not a natural person designated as its representative by its attorney;

   c. A person whose presence is shown by a party to be essential to the presentation of the party's cause; or

   d. A person authorized by statute to be present, such as a victim of the crime.

2. **General Principle.** The Apocrypha describes a case involving Susanna and the Elders. Two of the Elders, who had been appointed judges of the people, desired Susanna, a married woman. She rejected their propositions, and they decided to charge her with adultery. They testified before the people that they had seen Susanna with another man. Susanna was convicted of adultery and sentenced to death. Daniel interrupted the proceedings and told the people to separate the two men. Then he called them, one by one, and asked what kind of tree they were standing under when they saw Susanna with the other man. One Elder claimed it was an ash tree, while the other claimed it was a pear tree. In this way, Daniel saved Susanna and condemned the Elders of perjury by their own words.

# VIII. IMPEACHING WITNESSES

## A. INTRODUCTION

1.   **Effect of Impeachment.** To impeach a witness is to challenge the validity of the witness's testimony or to try to discredit the witness. The fact that a witness has been impeached does not mean that his testimony will be stricken or disregarded. The jury may still choose to believe the witness despite impeachment evidence.

2.   **Methods of Impeachment.** A witness's testimony may be discredited by:

   a.   **Rebuttal evidence.** The content of a witness's testimony may be rebutted by proof of facts contrary thereto.

   b.   **Evidence attacking credibility.** A witness's entire testimony may be discredited because his credibility as a witness is suspect.

   1)   **What constitutes.** The facts that the law recognizes as sufficient to attack credibility are the "grounds for impeachment." These grounds include sensory deficiencies (*e.g.*, mental capacity and lack of memory), poor character for truthfulness, bias or interest, and prior inconsistent statements.

   2)   **How proved.** Such grounds always may be brought out by examination of the witness, getting him to admit facts constituting impeachment. Certain of the grounds, such as criminal convictions, also may be proved by independent evidence.

## B. NONSPECIFIC IMPEACHMENT

1.   **Hostility, Bias, and Interest.** A witness may be impeached by showing that he is biased, hostile, or has some interest in the outcome of the trial giving him a motive to lie.

   a.   **Examples.**

   1)   **Compensation for testimony.** It is proper to ask a witness on cross-examination what compensation, etc., he has been promised for testifying. This might show that he is attempting to "earn" something by testifying in a particular manner.

   a)   **Example.** In criminal cases, it is proper to ask a prosecution witness on cross-examination whether there are any charges pending against him (or whether he is on parole or probation or awaiting sentencing), and whether he has been promised immunity or leniency on such charges.

2) **Bias of family and friends.**

a) **Family.** It always may be shown that the witness is related to one of the parties because this infers a bias in that party's favor. Otherwise, however, evidence as to the bias, prejudice, or interest of the witness's relatives generally is not admissible to impeach the witness. *Rationale:* A person cannot choose his relatives; hence, nothing can be inferred from their biases or interests.

b) **Friends.** On the other hand, a person can choose his friends and business associates, and consequently, evidence of their bias or interest generally is admissible for impeachment purposes.

3) **Hostility toward a party.** Hostility toward a party may be shown by adverse statements or by the fact that the witness has some dispute or litigation pending against the party.

b. **How proven and foundational requirement.** The bias, interest, or hostility of the witness can be proved either by cross-examination of the witness himself *or* by introducing extrinsic evidence *(e.g., testimony of other witnesses).* Most courts require that before a witness can be impeached by extrinsic evidence of bias, interest, or hostility, he must first be asked about the facts that indicate such bias, interest, or hostility. Only if the witness denies the bias, interest, or hostility will extrinsic evidence be admissible.

c. **Common membership in an organization as evidence of bias--**

---

**United States v. Abel,** 469 U.S. 45 (1984).

---

**Facts.** Abel (D), Ehle, and another were indicted for robbing a savings and loan. All pleaded guilty except D, and Ehle agreed to testify against D. D told the court that he planned to offer the testimony of Mills, a prison friend of D's and Ehle's, who claimed that Ehle had told him that he was going to implicate D falsely in the robbery to receive more favorable treatment. The prosecutor stated that he would then discredit Mills by having Ehle explain that he, D, and Mills were members of the Aryan Brotherhood, a secret prison gang that required its members to commit perjury, theft, and murder to protect one another. D objected to the rebuttal testimony, but the court permitted it as long as neither the name of the gang nor the punishments for violating its rules were disclosed. All of this evidence was presented at the trial, and D was convicted. On appeal, the Ninth Circuit Court of Appeals held that the suggestion of perjury based upon the group's tenet rather than on any evidence that Mills agreed with that tenet was reversible error. In other words, mere membership in the organization has no probative value as to Mills's credibility, and the evidence prejudiced D by mere association because D did not himself testify and could not therefore be impeached. The Supreme Court granted certiorari.

**Issue.** May a witness's bias be shown by extrinsic evidence, including membership in an organization the tenets of which include use of perjury to protect other members?

**Held.** Yes. Judgment reversed.

♦ The Federal Rules do not expressly deal with impeachment for bias, but they do clearly contemplate the use of bias, prejudice, or corruption as grounds of impeachment. Under Federal Rule 401, evidence is relevant if it has any tendency to make the existence of any fact that is of consequence to the determination of the action more probable or less probable than it would be without the evidence. A showing of bias on the part of a witness has a tendency to make the facts to which the witness testified less probable than it would be without such testimony; bias is thus relevant.

♦ Ehle's testimony about the gang was relevant because it made the existence of Mills's bias towards D more probable. Evidence law has traditionally permitted the showing of bias by extrinsic evidence even though less favored forms of impeachment could not be so proven.

♦ Mills's common membership with D in the gang is probative of bias. Mills's membership was not offered to convict either Mills or D of a crime, but to impeach Mills's testimony. It was not necessary for impeachment purposes to prove that Mills agreed with or adopted all of the tenets of the organization as it would have been if attempting to convict Mills based on adherence to those tenets.

♦ D claims that the court's allowing a description of the gang into evidence was unduly inflammatory and outweighed any probative value it may have had on Mills's bias. However, mutual membership in an organization is not meaningful without some description of the organization. The inference of bias varies depending on the type of organization involved; *i.e,* common membership in a book club would tend to show less bias than common membership in a prison gang. At any rate, the court properly exercised its discretion in balancing the competing interests by limiting the scope of the discussion of the organization.

---

2. **Capacity.**

   a. **Effect of mental disorders.** Several types of emotional or mental disorders may materially affect the accuracy of testimony, and therefore, evidence of such disorders has high probative value on the issue of credibility. For example, a paranoid person may interpret a reality skewed by suspicions, antipathies, or fantasies. A schizophrenic person may have difficulty distinguishing fact from fantasy and may have her memory distorted by delusions, hallucinations, and paranoid thinking.

    **b.**   **Basic rule.** Some courts allow a witness to be impeached by testimony from a treating physician as to the psychiatric condition of the witness being impeached. This type of impeachment usually involves testimony that a witness is a pathological liar. However, it may concern other mental conditions that would affect the credibility of the witness.

**3.**   **Character for Truthfulness.** Whenever a witness (party or nonparty) takes the stand, he puts his character for truthfulness in issue. Therefore, he can be impeached by evidence that his character is such that he may lie under oath. The difficult question is what evidence is admissible for this purpose.

    **a.**   **Nonconviction misconduct.** Prior bad acts, such as misconduct that has not been the subject of a criminal conviction, may still reflect on a witness's veracity.

        **1)**   **General view.** Most courts allow cross-examination as to prior bad acts if they are clearly probative of veracity and do not involve unreasonable risks of prejudice, confusion, etc. The judge has discretion in this area. [Fed. R. Evid. 608(b)] However, the examiner must be satisfied by the witness's answers; she cannot introduce extrinsic evidence to prove the past misconduct.

        **2)**   **Minority views.** The English view, which is followed by some courts, allows full inquiry into such misconduct on the theory that the entire personal history of a witness is "fair game" on cross-examination. Alternatively, some courts prohibit impeachment by this kind of evidence because when there is no criminal conviction, too many collateral issues are usually involved.

        **3)**   **Specific instances of conduct--**

---

**United States v. Manske,** 186 F.3d 770 (7th Cir. 1999).

---

**Facts.** Manske (D) was tried for conspiracy to distribute cocaine. Two of his co-offenders, Pszeniczka and Knutowski, identified D as their drug source, claiming that he sold them over five kilos of cocaine over three years. D admitted that he knew Pszeniczka and Knutowski, but claimed they engaged in sports betting and bookmaking only. D sought to cross-examine Pszeniczka about threats he had made to other witnesses on the theory that the threats demonstrated his willingness to dissuade people from testifying truthfully. The government objected and made a motion in limine to block this line of cross-examination. The trial court granted the motion. D was convicted. He appeals.

**Issue.** May a criminal defendant cross-examine a prosecution witness about the witness's willingness to threaten other witnesses with violence?

**Held.** Yes. Judgment reversed and case remanded.

- Rule 608(b) only allows the use of a witness's specific instances of conduct on cross-examination if they are probative of truthfulness or untruthfulness. The rule may be interpreted broadly, narrowly, or in between.

- The broad view treats virtually any conduct indicating bad character, including robbery and assault, as an indication of untruthfulness. It would allow the evidence D sought to use. However, this approach would swallow the rule because it is based on the notion that all bad people are liars. This approach should not be adopted.

- The narrow view would allow the use only of a witness's crimes involving falsehood or deception, such as forgery or perjury. This view probably would exclude D's evidence.

- The middle view concludes that a person's veracity is reflected by conduct seeking personal advantage by taking from others in violation of their rights. It would not necessarily exclude personal crimes involving violence.

- The trend is toward adopting the middle view. This allows cross-examination questions about a witness's prior acts of stealing, receiving stolen property, failure to file federal income tax returns, and bribery, on the theory that it is difficult to distinguish between untruthfulness and dishonesty.

- In this case, the relationship between the witness's specific acts of misconduct (threatening witnesses) and the witness's truthfulness is compelling. Threatening a witness is as probative of truthfulness as is receiving stolen tires (previous Seventh Circuit case allowed cross-examination about defendant's receipt of stolen tires). D should have been allowed to cross-examine Pszeniczka about his threatening of witnesses.

- D's theory that the other witnesses were biased against him because they feared for their personal safety is a separate ground for allowing this evidence as to those witnesses. D should have been allowed to ask them about their fear of Pszeniczka. D was not required to establish a foundation for bias-related questions. There are no special foundational requirements for bias evidence.

---

### b. Prior convictions.

1) **Introduction.** The early common law rule was that a person who had been convicted of a felony, or any misdemeanor involving dishonesty, was incompetent to testify at all. This rule has been abandoned, but proof of conviction of certain crimes may be used to impeach a witness. [Fed. R. Evid. 609]

2) **Which crimes.** The courts recognize that an instruction to the jury that it should consider a prior conviction only for impeachment, and not on the issue of guilt, is largely ineffective. Accordingly, the rules of evidence try to minimize the risk of prejudice by limiting the type of prior convictions that may be used for impeachment. The courts differ as to which crimes constitute grounds for impeachment.

   a) A number of states admit evidence of conviction of any crime, felony or misdemeanor.

   b) A few states limit impeachment to felonies and misdemeanors involving "moral turpitude" or "infamous" crimes.

   c) Other states hold that the crime must be one that would discredit the veracity or credibility of the witness, such as perjury, theft by false pretenses, etc.

   d) The probable majority view permits impeachment by any felony conviction, regardless of the type of offense committed.

   e) Rule 609(a) allows impeachment of any witness by any crime involving dishonesty or false statement, regardless of whether a felony or misdemeanor, and by any felony (crime punishable by death or imprisonment in excess of one year), provided that, if the accused is being impeached, the court determines that the probative value of admitting this evidence outweighs its prejudicial effect to the accused.

   f) Rule 609(b) provides that evidence of a conviction is not admissible if more than 10 years have elapsed since the date of conviction or the release of the witness from confinement, whichever is later, unless the court finds that the probative value of the conviction supported by specific facts and circumstances substantially outweighs its prejudicial effect.

3) **Inquiry into facts and circumstances--**

**United States v. Lipscomb**, 702 F.2d 1049 (D.C. Cir. 1983).

**Facts.** Lipscomb (D) was tried for possession of heroin. D testified, and the prosecution impeached him with evidence of a robbery conviction eight years previously. The trial ended in a hung jury. D was retried for the same crime. At his second trial, D moved to prevent cross-examination about the robbery, but the judge ruled that the prosecution could use the robbery conviction for cross-examination. D chose not to testify. The prosecution also used prior convictions to impeach three of D's defense witnesses. D was convicted. D moved for a new trial. The judge conducted a hearing on the motion, during which he heard additional evidence regarding the prior convictions. D appeals, claiming that the court should not have allowed the prior convictions to be used.

**Issue.** May a judge allow evidence of a defendant's prior conviction of robbery to be used as impeachment evidence if the defendant testifies at trial?

**Held.** Yes. Judgment affirmed.

♦ Under Rule 609(a)(1), when the prosecution seeks to use a defendant's prior felony conviction to impeach the defendant, the court is required to balance the probative value of the evidence against its prejudicial effect on the defendant. Under Rule 609(b), the court is required to look into specific facts and circumstances regarding a conviction that is more than 10 years old.

♦ The omission of a "facts and circumstances" requirement under Rule 609(a)(1) does not preclude a judge from looking into the facts and circumstances underlying a prior felony conviction. For one thing, the judge has to look into the facts to see if the conviction is 10 years old before Rule 609(b) comes into play. In addition, the judge needs to look into the facts and circumstances to determine whether the previous conviction involved dishonesty or false statement to bring it under Rule 609(a)(2). Moreover, it is appropriate to allow the court to consider facts in balancing probativeness against prejudice under Rule 609(a)(1). Thus, judges should have discretion to determine whether, and to what extent, to inquire into the facts and circumstances of prior convictions.

♦ In this case, the court discovered that although D's prior robbery conviction was for threatening a man with a B-B gun and taking $13 from the man and his hat and coat, D was subsequently arrested for burglary, failed to return to prison from an unescorted furlough, and was convicted of several other burglaries. The court's determination that the probative value of D's prior conviction outweighed the prejudicial effect on D was supported by the evidence. The court's determination regarding the prior convictions of D's witnesses also was supported by the evidence.

---

**4)    Defendant must testify to preserve claim of error on admission of prior conviction--**

**Luce v. United States,** 469 U.S. 38 (1984).

**Facts.** Luce (D) was tried for conspiracy and possession of cocaine with intent to distribute. D moved for a ruling to prevent the prosecution from using a prior conviction to impeach him if he testified, but D did not commit to testify if the court granted the motion, and he did not describe what his testimony would be. The prosecution argued that the prior conviction for possession of a controlled substance was a serious crime. The court ruled that the conviction fell within Rule 609(a) as proper impeachment evidence and could be used to impeach D if he took the stand, unless he limited his testimony to explaining his attempt to escape from the arresting officers—*i.e.,* D could not testify that he had no prior involvement with drugs or the prior conviction would be admissible. D did not testify. D was convicted. The Sixth Circuit affirmed, and the Supreme Court granted certiorari.

**Issue.** May a defendant who did not testify at trial appeal the court's denial of his motion to prohibit the prosecution's use of a prior conviction to impeach his credibility?

**Held.** No. Judgment affirmed.

♦ Had D testified and been impeached by the prior conviction, the court's decision to permit the impeachment would have been reviewable on appeal. The appellate court must have a complete record in order to weigh the probative value of a prior conviction against the prejudicial effect to D. When D does not testify, the possible harm of the ruling is speculative. Also, the court cannot be sure that the prosecution would have even used the impeachment evidence.

♦ The difficulties of assessing a ruling when D does not testify are bad enough, but to permit review of an in limine ruling under Federal Rule 609(a) would result in automatic reversal because a ruling that presumably keeps D from testifying could hardly be considered harmless. Reviewing courts can only review a 609(a) claim when D preserves the claim by testifying.

---

c. **Poor reputation for truthfulness.** Because the witness's credibility is always at issue, he may be impeached by showing that he has a poor reputation in the community for truthfulness.

## C. SPECIFIC IMPEACHMENT

1. **Prior Inconsistent Statements.** A witness also may be impeached (discredited) by showing that he has made prior inconsistent statements regarding the matters as to which he has given testimony.

a. **Actual inconsistency required.** Before a witness's prior inconsistent statement can be admitted, it must in fact be inconsistent with his testimony at trial. Thus, if the witness's only testimony is that he does not remember anything, the prior statement is inadmissible because there is nothing with which it can be inconsistent.

b. **Laying a foundation.** There is a split of authority as to whether the prior inconsistent statement can be introduced directly into evidence, or whether the witness must first be asked about the statement and be given an opportunity to explain the inconsistency.

   1) **Traditional rule.** The traditional rule requires that the witness be asked about the statement before it can be introduced; *i.e.*, the cross-examiner must ask the witness whether he made the statement (giving its substance), and must name the time, place, and person to whom it was made. If the statement was in writing, the cross-examiner must also show the witness the writing or a copy thereof.

   2) **Criticism of traditional rule.** The rationale for the traditional rule is to avoid unfair surprise to the witness (and the party calling him). However, the procedure is criticized because it always alerts the witness to the possible impeachment and gives him an opportunity to talk around the damaging evidence, possibly further concealing the truth.

   3) **Modern rules limit foundational questioning**. Recognizing the validity of the above criticism, many jurisdictions today limit the foundational questions that must be asked. Under the modern rules, extrinsic evidence of a prior inconsistent statement will be admissible if the witness is, *at some point*, given an opportunity to explain or deny the allegedly inconsistent statement. [Fed. R. Evid. 613(b); Cal. Evid. Code §770(a)] The opportunity need not come before introduction of the statement.

c. **Evidentiary effect of statement.**

   1) **Majority rule.** The traditional (and still majority) rule is that a prior inconsistent statement by the witness is hearsay, and therefore cannot be used as proof of the facts contained therein (unless it qualifies under some exception to the hearsay rule). The use of a prior inconsistent statement is limited to impeachment of the witness, and the jury must be so instructed.

   2) **Minority rule.** A few jurisdictions have now rejected the above rule and admit a prior inconsistent statement as substantive proof of the matters contained therein. [*See, e.g.*, Cal. Evid. Code §1235]

a)  **Hearsay status.** The jurisdictions that follow this approach recognize a special exception to the hearsay rule for prior inconsistent statements made by witnesses who testify at trial. [*See, e.g.,* Cal. Evid. Code §1235]

b)  **Rationale.** There is no real hearsay problem because the declarant is in court and may be cross-examined with regard to the statement. Also, the prior statement will often be more accurate than in-court testimony because it was made nearer to the time of the events in question. Furthermore, telling the jury to consider the statement for "impeachment purposes only" is simply asking too much of the jurors.

3)  **Federal Rules.** Under the Federal Rules, a prior inconsistent statement is in most instances admissible solely for impeachment purposes (as under the majority view). However, the Federal Rules recognize one limited exception: a prior inconsistent statement made by a witness while testifying under oath at some prior trial, hearing, or other proceeding is admissible nonhearsay; as such, it can be used as substantive proof of whatever was stated. [Fed. R. Evid. 801(d)(1)]

4)  **Good faith limitation--**

---

## United States v. Webster, 734 F.2d 1191 (7th Cir. 1984).

---

**Facts.** Webster (D) was tried for aiding and abetting a bank robbery. The prosecution called the bank robber (W), now serving a long sentence on his guilty plea to testify against D. When examined by the prosecution, D gave testimony exculpating D. Over D's objection, the prosecution then introduced W's prior inconsistent statements to the FBI. The district court instructed the jury that the statements could be used only to impeach W and not as evidence of D's guilt. D was convicted. D appeals.

**Issue.** May a prosecution's witness be cross-examined by the prosecution with a prior inconsistent statement that implicates the defendant?

**Held.** Yes. Judgment affirmed.

♦   Although the party calling a witness may attack the witness's credibility (Federal Rule 607), and credibility may be attacked by evidence of prior inconsistent statements (Federal Rule 613), the prosecution may not get inadmissible evidence before the jury by calling a witness it knows to be hostile and then using his out-of-court statements, which would otherwise be inadmissible hearsay, to impeach him.

♦   Here, however, the prosecutor appears, in good faith, not to have known that W's testimony would be unfavorable. She asked the judge to allow her to examine W outside the presence of the jury because she did not know what he would say. D's counsel objected, and the voir dire was not held.

**Comment.** It is unclear what D's counsel expected to gain by preventing the voir dire examination of W. D urged that the government ought to show both surprise and harm before it can introduce the prior inconsistent statements of a turncoat witness, but the Seventh Circuit rejected the idea.

---

    d.    **Use of illegally obtained evidence for impeachment purposes.** As a general rule, illegally obtained evidence is inadmissible for any purpose. However, an exception has been made in certain narrow circumstances involving the impeachment of a defendant's testimony when he appears to be committing perjury (based on the illegally obtained evidence).

    e.    **Voluntary confession obtained in violation of *Miranda*--**

---

## Harris v. New York, 401 U.S. 222 (1971).

---

**Facts.** Harris (D) was being prosecuted for selling heroin on two occasions to an undercover police officer. After arrest and prior to trial, in violation of D's constitutional rights (as set forth in the *Miranda* case concerning custodial interrogation), D made statements concerning the sale of drugs by him to the undercover officer. At trial, D took the stand and testified that he never sold heroin to the officer. The prosecution then offered evidence concerning D's statements after his arrest. The purpose of the evidence was to contradict D's testimony that he never made the sale. The trial court instructed the jury that this testimony was to be considered only in deciding D's credibility. D was convicted. The New York Court of Appeals affirmed. The Supreme Court granted certiorari.

**Issue.** May statements made by a defendant that are otherwise inadmissible be used to impeach the defendant's credibility if he testifies at his trial?

**Held.** Yes. Judgment affirmed.

♦    A statement obtained in violation of the *Miranda* rule, although inadmissible against D as part of the prosecution's case on guilt, may be used to impeach D's testimony if he takes the stand at trial, provided that the statement is otherwise voluntary and trustworthy under proper legal standards.

♦    Every criminal defendant has the right to testify if he so chooses, but he does not have the right to testify falsely. The shield provided by *Miranda* cannot be perverted into a license to use perjury by way of a defense, free from the risk of confrontation with prior inconsistent utterances, even though unlawfully obtained.

**Dissent** (Brennan, Douglas, Marshall, JJ.). The choice to testify in one's own defense must be "unfettered." Thus, it cannot be burdened by the risk that an illegally obtained prior statement may be used for impeachment purposes.

---

### f.    Pre-arrest silence--

## Jenkins v. Anderson, 447 U.S. 231 (1980).

**Facts.** Jenkins (D) stabbed and killed Redding the day after Redding had robbed D's sister and her boyfriend. Immediately after the robbery, D, who was nearby, followed Redding and disclosed Redding's location to the police. The next day, D encountered Redding, and Redding accused D of reporting him to the police. During this encounter, D stabbed and killed Redding and did not turn himself in to the police for two weeks thereafter. At D's trial, he testified that Redding had attacked him, and that he had stabbed Redding in self-defense. On cross-examination, the prosecutor elicited D's admission that he did not report the stabbing to the police for two weeks. In closing arguments, the prosecutor also reminded the jury that D waited two weeks before reporting the incident, suggesting that D had not acted in self-defense. D was convicted of manslaughter and sentenced to 10 to 15 years' imprisonment. D sought federal habeas corpus relief. The lower courts denied relief, and the Supreme Court granted certiorari.

**Issue.** May a defendant's pre-arrest silence be used to impeach him if he testifies at his trial?

**Held.** Yes. Judgment affirmed.

♦     The Court held in *Raffel v. United States*, 271 U.S. 494 (1926) that the right to remain silent is not infringed when a defendant's own prior silence is used for impeachment of his testimony. A defendant who testifies is subject to cross-examination impeaching his credibility just like any other witness.

♦     *Harris, supra*, reiterated the basic rule, noting that while a criminal defendant is privileged to refuse to testify, if he chooses to testify, he has no right to commit perjury. Once he takes the stand, a defendant has an obligation to speak truthfully, and the prosecution can use the normal truth-testing devices of the adversary process, including impeachment.

♦     In *Doyle v. Ohio*, 426 U.S. 610 (1976), the Court held that a defendant's silence cannot be used for impeachment when the defendant, after having been advised of his *Miranda* rights, chooses not to say anything. The difference between *Doyle* and this case is that here, no government action induced D to remain silent before his arrest.

---

2.  **Contradiction.**

    a.  **Basic rule.** A witness may be impeached by evidence that contradicts her testimony. Such contradictory evidence is called counterproof. It is normally admissible only if it has some relevance in addition to contradicting the witness, such as when the counterproof tends to prove a point in the case in addition to contradicting the witness. If the sole utility of the counterproof is to contradict the witness, it is considered "collateral" and not admitted. The rationale for this limitation is that otherwise, the examination could go far astray from the issues in the case.

    b.  **Contradicting statements made during cross-examination--**

---

## United States v. Havens, 446 U.S. 620 (1980).

---

**Facts.** Havens (D) was convicted of importing and possessing cocaine. Havens and a traveling companion took a flight from Lima, Peru to Miami, Florida. In Miami, a customs officer searched D's companion and found cocaine sewn into makeshift pockets in a T-shift the companion was wearing. The companion implicated D who had previously cleared customs. D was arrested, and customs officers seized and searched his luggage without a warrant. The officers did not find cocaine but did find a cut-up T-shirt; the cut-out pieces matched those sewn into D's companion's T-shirt. At trial, D denied on direct examination that he had ever been involved in smuggling drugs. On cross-examination, D denied knowledge of having a T-shirt with missing pieces in his luggage. The prosecution then introduced the seized T-shirt to rebut D's credibility. The court of appeals reversed D's conviction, holding that illegally obtained evidence could be used for impeachment only of a statement made in direct examination. The Supreme Court granted certiorari.

**Issue.** May illegally obtained evidence be used to impeach statements made by a defendant during a cross-examination that is reasonably suggested by the direct examination?

**Held.** Yes. Judgment reversed and case remanded.

♦   Attempts by the prosecution to admit illegally obtained evidence by bringing out testimony for the first time on cross-examination and then rebutting it with the illegally obained evidence violate the defendant's rights and are prohibited.

However, this does not mean that only statements on direct examination may be rebutted.

♦ The exclusionary rule is not a license to use perjury by way of defense. If the cross-examination is reasonably suggested by the direct examination, then statements by the defendant may be rebutted with illegally obtained evidence.

**Dissent** (Brennan, Marshall, Stewart, Stevens, JJ.). This new rule allows a reasonably talented prosecutor to work in evidence on cross-examination that is suppressed because of illegal police conduct. This will compel D to forgo testifying on his own behalf.

---

## D. REPAIRING CREDIBILITY

1. **Rehabilitation by Explanation on Redirect.** If a witness was impeached on cross-examination, the witness always is allowed on redirect to explain the facts brought out on cross-examination.

2. **Rehabilitation with Character Evidence.**

   a. **General rule.** When a witness's character for truth and veracity has been attacked, the party for whom the impeached witness has testified may call other witnesses to testify to the impeached witness's good reputation for truth or to give their opinion as to the impeached witness's truthfulness. [Fed. R. Evid. 608(a)]

   b. **Use of character witnesses--**

---

**United States v. Medical Therapy Sciences,** 583 F.2d 36 (2d Cir. 1978).

---

**Facts.** Medical Therapy Sciences (D) was charged with filing false Medicare claims. At trial, the government contended that D devised a scheme to double bill insurance companies for the same patients, to charge the insurance companies for more expensive equipment than was provided, and to bill the insurance companies for supplies that were not provided. To prove this contention, the government called Russell (W), an employee of D who supervised much of D's billing. W testified that she discussed the rules and practices of the company with D's owner and both knew that they were collecting funds to which D was not entitled. D cross-examined W in regard to her prior convictions that the government brought out on W's direct examination and her bias against D; the government had asked W on direct about D's claim that W embezzled money from it and stole patients when she established a competing business, and W denied this claim. On rebuttal, the government introduced character witnesses, over D's objection, to bolster W's credibility. D was convicted and appeals.

**Issue.** Once a witness's credibility is impeached on cross-examination, may that witness's credibility be rehabilitated with testimony from character witnesses?

**Held.** Yes. Judgment affirmed.

♦ Rule 608(a)(2) provides that "evidence of truthful character is admissible only after the character of the witness for truthfulness has been attacked by opinion or reputation evidence or otherwise."

♦ W was cross-examined both about her prior convictions and about specific acts of misconduct. Although the government made this a close question by first eliciting testimony (on direct) of W's prior convictions and her alleged acts of misconduct, the trial court had discretion either to admit or to exclude rebuttal evidence of W's good character for truthfulness.

♦ The trial court has discretion to permit rehabilitation under circumstances when, subsequent to the revelation of a witness's problems on direct examination, the opponent paints the witness with more accusatory strokes—especially where, as here, wrongdoing which implicates veracity is alleged and denied.

---

3. **Rehabilitation with Prior Consistent Statement.**

    a. **General rule—inadmissible.** Most courts hold that evidence of a witness's prior consistent statement (consistent with his direct testimony) is not admissible to rehabilitate him after he has been impeached by proof of a prior inconsistent statement.

        1) **Rationale.** There is no way of telling when the witness was lying.

        2) **Exceptions.** There are, however, a number of exceptions to this rule.

            a) **Witness denies inconsistent statement.** If the witness denies ever having made the inconsistent statement, evidence of a prior consistent statement has been held admissible to bolster his denial, although there is less unanimity among the cases on this point.

            b) **Witness's memory attacked.** Similarly, when the accuracy of the witness's memory has been attacked on cross-examination, a number of decisions allow proof of a prior consistent statement made at or shortly after the event in question to prove that his testimony on direct is more likely correct than some intervening, inconsistent statement made by him.

c) **"Recent contrivance doctrine."** When the impeachment suggests that the witness's testimony on direct was recently fabricated (*e.g.,* induced by counsel), or otherwise colored by some improper motive, proof of a consistent statement made by the witness before the alleged motive to fabricate arose is admissible to disprove that the direct testimony was so contrived or motivated. [Fed. R. Evid. 801(d)(1)(B); Cal. Evid. Code §791(b)]

# IX. OPINION AND EXPERT TESTIMONY; SCIENTIFIC EVIDENCE

## A. LAY OPINION

1.  **Introduction.** An opinion is an inference from facts observed. The general rule is that the drawing of such inferences is the function of the trier of fact, and hence, testimony that is the mere opinion or conclusion of the witness is not admissible. Nevertheless, in some situations, statements that are conclusions or opinions by the witness are admissible. In some fields, the opinions must be given by properly qualified experts. In others, opinions by lay witnesses are admitted.

2.  **Opinion Evidence by Lay Witnesses.** Conclusions and opinions by lay witnesses are admissible when they are derived from the witnesses' personal observation of the facts in issue and when, from the nature of those facts, no better evidence thereof can be obtained.

3.  **Requirements for Admissibility.** Before a lay witness's opinion is admissible, the trial judge must be satisfied that both of the following elements are satisfied.

    a.  The witness's opinion is "rationally based on the perception of the witness" (*i.e.,* the witness personally observed that about which he has an opinion).

    b.  The opinion is "helpful to a clear understanding of the witness's testimony or the determination of a fact in issue." This generally means that the subject matter of the witness's opinion is something about which normal persons regularly form opinions (*e.g.,* speed, size, sound, etc.), and that testimony in the form of an opinion is the clearest way of getting the matter to the jury. *Example:* a witness testifying that a person looked "drunk" may be a clearer way of conveying the person's appearance to the jury than describing details as to his manner of speech, smell of his breath, etc. [Fed. R. Evid. 701]

## B. EXPERT WITNESSES

1.  **Requirements for Admissibility—In General.** Before a witness is permitted to give opinion testimony as an expert, the trial court must determine the following:

    a.  **Specialized knowledge helpful to jury.** First of all, it must appear that the subject matter at issue goes beyond the everyday knowledge of persons of ordinary experience and education; *i.e.,* that some scientific, technical, or other specialized knowledge would be of assistance to the trier of fact in understanding the evidence or determining the issue.

b. **Witness specially qualified**. It must appear that the witness whose opinion is offered has some special knowledge, skill, experience, or other qualification that would be of assistance to the jury for the purpose aforesaid.

c. **Proper basis for opinion.** Finally, the witness's opinion must be based on matters that experts in the particular field reasonably rely upon in forming opinions regarding the subject matter at issue (*see* below). [Fed. R. Evid. 702, 703]

d. **Preliminary fact question for judge**. The trial court's determination of whether a witness can give opinion testimony as an expert is one of the preliminary matters as to which the proponent carries the burden of persuasion; *i.e.,* unless the trial court is persuaded as to the witness's qualifications, etc., the opinion testimony is not admissible.

e. **Expert testimony occasionally mandatory.** Usually, expert testimony is merely one method by which a party may prove its case. However, sometimes expert testimony will be required *as a matter of law*; *i.e.,* when the subject matter is such that the jurors cannot determine liability from common experience, a nonsuit must be granted unless qualified expert testimony is introduced to support the claim of liability.

2. **Procedure.** Unless the expert witness is shown to have personally perceived the facts (*e.g.,* the treating physician), most courts require the expert to disclose the facts or data upon which he relied in forming his opinion ***before*** he states his opinion. Such statement of fact or data may be elicited from the expert witness in either of the following manners.

a. **Testimony heard in court.** The expert may be asked if he was in court and heard the facts as developed by previous testimony, and whether his opinion is based thereon.

b. **Hypothetical question.** A hypothetical question may be posed for the expert. (In many states, this is the only way in which expert testimony may be received.) A hypothetical question is one that asks the expert witness to assume as true various data that examining counsel believes he has proved (or will be able to prove) concerning the condition in question and then asks the expert to state an opinion based on the assumed data.

c. **Federal rule.** Note that under the Federal Rules, a witness may give an opinion *without* first revealing the basis of her opinion, unless otherwise required by the court. [Fed. R. Evid. 705]

# C. RELIABILITY STANDARDS FOR SCIENTIFIC EVIDENCE

1. **Definition.** Generally, "scientific evidence" refers to experiments that are conducted out of court and the results thereof described at trial by witnesses. An example is tests to see what distance a certain type of brake can stop a car going at a variety of speeds.

2. **Problems of Admissibility.**

   a. **Relevancy.** The biggest problem usually is one of relevancy.

      1) The conditions under which the experiment is conducted must be substantially similar to the facts that existed at the time that the events in dispute occurred. For example, if an experiment is conducted to show that a bullet could have pierced a metal sheet, the metal used, the type of gun, the distance of the gun from the target, etc., must be shown to be substantially identical.

      2) In many instances, when the experiment involved is technical and complex, the witness describing the experiment will have to be a qualified expert. Second, whether the witness is an expert or lay witness, the witness must describe the test, the conclusions and reasons therefor, and the accuracy of the results. However, when a test has become established as reliable (X-rays, fingerprints, etc.), judicial notice will be taken of its accuracy.

   b. **Substitute for relevancy.** The modern trend is to speak about relevancy when discussing whether a test or experiment will help clarify the issues involved. However, in the past, some courts have used another rationale; *i.e.,* that the test concerned did not yield admissible evidence because it had not as yet received "general scientific acceptance." Whether a test is reliable (and thus probative and helpful) is clearly an issue, but one that should be discussed under the traditional heading of "relevancy."

   c. **Prejudicial evidence.** Even if a test or experiment yields relevant evidence, such evidence may be excluded in the discretion of the judge due to its prejudicial nature. This generally is what happens with evidence derived by putting a witness under hypnosis or the influence of "truth" drugs, etc.

3. **Specific Tests or Experiments.**

   a. **Radar test to measure speed.** When radar is used to measure the speed of a moving car, this evidence will be admitted if a foundation is first laid as to the accuracy of the device itself and its operation.

b. **Body fluid tests.** Chemical tests for intoxication (blood, urine, etc.), whether voluntarily or involuntarily given, are usually admitted. Blood tests to prove identity, such as when an accused's blood type is found on a victim's clothing, are also usually admissible. Blood tests for paternity are discussed *supra.*

c. **Lie detector tests.** Generally, lie detector tests are not admissible in evidence because they are thought to be untrustworthy. However, when such tests are administered by a qualified expert, some courts will admit the evidence if all parties agree to have the tests taken.

d. **Human epidemiological studies--**

---

## Daubert v. Merrell Dow Pharmaceuticals, Inc., 509 U.S. 579 (1993).

---

**Facts.** Daubert (P) was born with birth defects. P, another child, and their parents sued Merrell Dow Pharmaceuticals, Inc. (D), alleging that the drug Bendectin which P's mother and the other child's mother ingested while they were pregnant and which D marketed caused the birth defects. D moved for summary judgment based on an affidavit by an expert who had reviewed all the literature on the relationship between Bendectin and human birth defects. The epidemiological studies involved over 130,000 patients and found no case in which Bendectin was capable of causing birth defects. P offered the testimony of eight experts who concluded that Bendectin can cause birth defects, based on various studies on animal cells and chemical structure and a reanalysis of previously published studies. The court granted D's motion for summary judgment on the ground that P's evidence was not sufficiently established to have gained general acceptance in the field. The court of appeals affirmed, noting that P's reanalysis of published studies had never been published or subjected to peer review. The Supreme Court granted certiorari.

**Issue.** Is expert scientific testimony admissible in federal court only if it satisfies the *Frye* test?

**Held.** No. Judgment vacated and case remanded.

♦ The "general acceptance" test was developed in *Frye v. United States,* 293 F. 1013 (D.C. Cir. 1923). It provided that expert testimony deduced from a well-recognized scientific principle or discovery is admissible only when the thing from which the deduction is made is sufficiently established to have gained general acceptance in the particular field in which it belongs.

♦ P claims that the *Frye* test was superseded by the Federal Rules of Evidence. Federal Rule 402 provides that all relevant evidence is admissible, except as otherwise provided; Federal Rule 401 provides that "relevant evidence" is that which has any tendency to make the existence of any fact that is of consequence to the determination of the action more probable or less probable than it would be without the evidence. The *Frye* test is inconsistent with this liberal approach to relevance.

♦ Rule 702 specifically governs expert testimony and states that if specialized knowledge will assist the trier of fact to understand the evidence, a qualified expert can testify about it. There is no requirement for "general acceptance" as an absolute prerequisite to admissibility. Thus, if the subject of an expert's testimony is "scientific, technical, or other specialized knowledge," it should be admitted if it is relevant. To qualify as "scientific knowledge," an inference or assertion must be derived by the scientific method.

♦ A court deciding whether to admit expert scientific testimony must first determine whether the expert is proposing to testify to (i) scientific knowledge that (ii) will assist the trier of fact to understand or determine a fact in issue. Important factors for the court to consider include whether the theory or technique: (i) can be, and has been, tested; (ii) has been subjected to peer review and publication; and (iii) has standards controlling its operation. The court also should consider the known or potential rate of error. General acceptance can be relevant, but is not a mandatory precondition to admissibility.

**Comment.** The use of expert witnesses as "hired guns" has expanded greatly in recent years. An expert can be found to support virtually any proposition, and there are many professional witnesses whose primary business is testifying and helping to prepare cases. It is increasingly difficult for courts to determine what type of evidence is truly "scientific."

---

e. **Application of *Daubert* to technical knowledge--**

# Kumho Tire Company, Ltd. v. Carmichael, 526 U.S. 137 (1998).

**Facts.** A tire on Carmichael's (P's) car blew out as he was driving. This led to one passenger's death and serious injuries to other passengers. P sued the tire manufacturer, Kumho Tire Company, Ltd. (D). P's expert witness, Carlson, was an expert in tire failure analysis who intended to testify that the tire was defective. The trial court applied the *Daubert* analysis and excluded the evidence. The court of appeals reversed, holding that *Daubert* was limited to the scientific context and thus did not apply to Carlson's testimony, which was based on his skill and experience. The Supreme Court granted certiorari.

**Issue.** Does the *Daubert* analysis apply to the testimony of engineers and other experts who are not scientists?

**Held.** Yes. Judgment reversed.

♦ Under *Daubert,* a trial court must make a "gatekeeping" determination when a party seeks to introduce scientific knowledge. The purpose of the *Daubert* factors was to assure that evidence is reliable as well as relevant. This objective applies as much to expert witnesses as it does to scientific evidence. There is no reason for trial courts to distinguish between "scientific" knowledge and "technical" knowledge. Therefore, *Daubert's* general principles apply to expert testimony under Federal Rule of Evidence 702.

♦ The factors set forth in *Daubert* were meant to be helpful, not definitive. A trial court has discretion to apply them as appropriate or to apply other factors that test reliability of the offered evidence. The trial court must have latitude in deciding how to test an expert's reliability.

♦ In this case, the trial court determined that Carlson's testimony was not reliable. The issue was the reasonableness of using Carlson's particular method of analyzing tire malfunctions to determine the cause of tire separation. Carlson's depositions cast considerable doubt on the reliability of both the explicit theory he applied and the implicit proposition about the significance of visual inspection. The court did not abuse its discretion in this case.

**Concurrence** (Scalia, O'Connor, Thomas, JJ.). The trial court must choose among reasonable means of excluding expertise that is unreliable. The discretion of the court to choose the manner of testing expert reliability does not include discretion to perform the gatekeeping function inadequately.

**Concurrence and dissent** (Stevens, J.). Whether Carlson should have been allowed to testify should be decided by the trial court under the correct standard set out in this opinion.

---

4. **Modern Science in the Courtroom.**

   a. **Introduction.** Advances in basic science and technology have made forensic evidence increasingly important in the trial process. The science of blood typing, human tissue analysis, and DNA analysis has entered the popular culture to the point that many juries expect the lawyers to present detailed scientific evidence in cases when it is relevant. Science plays a big role in resolving toxic tort cases, and behavioral syndromes such as the battered child and battered spouse syndromes are becoming more important in criminal cases.

   b. **DNA evidence--**

**State v. Moore**, 885 P.2d 457 (Mont. 1994).

**Facts.** Moore (D) was charged with the murder of a man whose body was never found. Human muscle and brain tissue was found in the cab of D's truck, and witnesses testified that D was supposed to have been with the victim about the time the victim disappeared. Over D's objection, the court admitted DNA analysis of the tissue, including RFLP and PCR analysis. Expert testimony showed that the tissue could not be excluded as having come from the father of the victim's children. D was convicted. D appeals.

**Issue.** Is DNA evidence sufficiently reliable to be used as evidence in a criminal trial?

**Held.** Yes. Judgment affirmed.

♦ A human DNA molecule contains about three billion base pairs. Genetically, humans are more alike than dissimilar, and nearly 99% of human DNA molecules are the same. Only about three million base pairs are in variable regions, called "polymorphisms." These account for the distinctions between individuals. The length of each polymorphism depends on the number of repeat core sequences of base pairs. The total fragment length is called a Restriction Fragment Length Polymorphism ("RFLP"). Alternative forms of RFLPs are called alleles.

♦ RFLP analysis involves using chemical enzymes to extract the DNA from the tissue sample. The DNA is then severed at targeted locations to create fragments containing polymorphic DNA segments. These segments are sorted electrically by length before they are transferred to a membrane. From there, the segments are processed to create a pattern of bands that are distinct for each person. This is the DNA print that can be used to compare tissue samples.

♦ Statistical analysis is then used to determine the likelihood that a match is unique. Statisticians figure out the frequency with which each particular allele is found in the total population, then calculate an aggregate estimate of the probability that D's combination of alleles would be found in the relevant racial population.

♦ Although there are problems with DNA evidence, the use of this type of evidence satisfies the *Daubert* standard.

**Comment.** Once a jurisdiction has approved a type of scientific evidence such as DNA testing, the proponent of the evidence must still prove that a particular laboratory's techniques are valid. Then the proponent must show that in a particular case, the laboratory correctly performed the test. Due to the complexity of these tests, there are several things that can go wrong. In addition, there are potential problems with the statistical analysis part of DNA testing, such as deciding what is the relevant population.

# X. BURDENS OF PROOF AND PRESUMPTIONS

## A. CIVIL CASES

1. **Introduction—Burden of Proof.** Except when the court takes judicial notice of a fact, the fact finder—whether judge or jury—must rely on the parties to produce evidence sufficient to persuade one way or the other. This section discusses problems of which party must present evidence, how much evidence must be presented, and the effect of that presentation. The term "burden of proof" actually refers to two separate concepts:

   a. **Burden of persuasion.** "Burden of proof" is most commonly used to describe the extent of a party's obligation to produce evidence to prove the facts. It is the obligation of a party to establish by evidence a requisite degree of belief in the mind of the trier of fact. The fact finder determines whether this burden is satisfied and renders a verdict accordingly.

      1) **Quantum of evidence required.**

         a) **Preponderance of evidence.** The general burden of persuasion in civil cases is the preponderance of evidence standard. It applies to almost all issues in civil cases, to preliminary fact determinations made by the judge, and even to some issues in criminal cases such as venue and statute of limitations.

            (1) **Definition.** The preponderance of evidence standard has been described as requiring such evidence as, when weighed against that opposed to it, has more convincing force, and is thus more believable. It is essentially a balancing; whichever side produces the greater weight of evidence satisfies the burden.

            (2) **Effect.** The party having the burden of persuasion must produce a preponderance of evidence to persuade the fact finder. That party cannot prevail if it produces evidence equal to the opposing side.

         b) **Clear and convincing evidence.** For certain types of issues, a proponent must present clear and convincing evidence, a higher burden than the preponderance of evidence standard. Typically, fraud allegations must be proven by clear and convincing evidence. If the case involves a severe sanction, but still short of a criminal conviction, this higher standard may apply; *e.g.,* denaturalization of a citizen, disbarment of an attorney, etc.

**b. Burden of going forward.** A party has an obligation of introducing or going forward with the evidence if that party bears the burden of persuasion as to that issue. Failure to satisfy this burden by introducing legally sufficient evidence may result in a directed verdict against the party with the burden. This burden is required because if neither party presented any evidence on an issue, the issue could not be decided.

    **1) Requirements.** A party satisfies the burden of going forward with evidence by introducing legally sufficient evidence on the issue, evidence that would allow a jury to decide the issue. If the party meets its burden of persuasion after satisfying the burden of going forward with the evidence, it would win a judgment. If the party fails to go forward with the evidence, the court may direct a verdict against the party as to that issue, which in turn could result in a directed verdict for the whole case.

    **2) Shift of burden.** Normally, the plaintiff has the burden of going forward as to all of the allegations in the complaint. Once the plaintiff has done so, the defendant has three basic options.

        a) Offer no evidence, relying on the plaintiff's failure to meet the burden of persuasion;

        b) Introduce evidence to contradict or undermine the plaintiff's evidence, thus persuading the fact finder that the plaintiff did not meet the burden of persuasion; and

        c) Introduce evidence of affirmative defenses such as contributory negligence. The defendant assumes the burden of persuasion and the burden of going forward as to affirmative defenses.

## 2. Presumptions.

**a. Introduction.** The law may require the fact finder to make a deduction from particular facts in evidence in the absence of a contrary showing. This legal device is called a presumption. It has the effect of shifting the burden of going forward with the evidence; it imposes on the party against whom it is directed the burden of going forward with evidence to meet or rebut the presumption. This is essentially a procedural tool. However, in diversity cases involving a claim or defense under state law, the federal courts deem the burden of proof a substantive matter for *Erie* doctrine purposes and so apply state law presumptions. Presumptions may be characterized as either conclusive or rebuttable.

b. **Procedure.** Before a presumption takes effect, the proponent must establish the basic fact that is a condition to the presumed fact. If the basic fact is disputed, the fact finder must make findings as to that fact before the presumption can arise. For example, if by statute a person missing for seven years is presumed dead, the proponent must prove that the person has been missing for seven years before the fact finder may presume that the person is dead.

c. **Effect of rebuttable presumptions.** Rebuttable presumptions have the effect of placing upon the opposing party the burden of going forward with the evidence. If the opposing party does so, the case goes to the fact finder. There is a divergence of views as to what happens to the presumption in such a situation.

  1) **Presumption is evidence.** Some jurisdictions hold that a presumption is evidence, so that even if contrary evidence is presented, the fact finder can weigh the presumption against the conflicting evidence. However, this is a theoretically difficult view because it allows the jury to weigh a legal conclusion against evidence.

  2) **Presumption not evidence.** Most courts agree that a presumption is not evidence, but a deduction that the fact finder must draw from particular evidence unless contradicted. Once contradicted, there are various approaches that these courts take to the situation.

    a) **Presumption dispelled.** Most courts hold that a presumption is merely a preliminary assumption of fact that disappears once contrary evidence is introduced. Rule 301 follows this approach, except that in diversity cases, state laws are followed.

    b) **Presumption not dispelled.** Other authorities contend that a presumption remains until the opposing party produces sufficiently strong evidence against the presumption as to persuade the fact finder that the presumption is not true.

    c) **Mixed effect.** Another approach, adopted by California, makes the effect of the counter evidence depend on the type of presumption involved. Under this approach, presumptions designed to implement public policy remain, but others do not.

d. **Conclusive presumptions.** Because conclusive presumptions are rules of substantive law, they cannot be contradicted by contrary evidence or arguments over logic. Many of these presumptions are statutory.

e.    **Shifting burdens--**

---

## Texas Department of Community Affairs v. Burdine, 450 U.S. 248 (1981).

---

**Facts.** Burdine (P), a female, worked for the Texas Department of Community Affairs (D). A male from another division of D was promoted instead of P, and P was fired. Although P was later rehired at a higher salary, she brought a gender discrimination suit under Title VII of the Civil Rights Act. The district court found for D, but the court of appeals reversed. The Supreme Court granted certiorari to consider the correct standard of proof.

**Issue.** Does the plaintiff in a discrimination suit retain the ultimate burden of persuading the trier of fact that the defendant intentionally discriminated against the plaintiff?

**Held.** Yes. Judgment vacated and case remanded.

◆      P has the initial burden of proving a prima facie case of discrimination; *i.e.*, that she was rejected for a position under circumstances that give rise to an inference of unlawful discrimination. This effectively creates a presumption that D did unlawfully discriminate.

◆      Once a prima facie case is established, the burden shifts to D to produce evidence that its action was based on a legitimate, nondiscriminatory reason. This burden is satisfied if D's evidence raises a genuine issue of fact about the discrimination. Thus, the presumption is rebutted.

◆      At this point, the burden shifts back to P to prove that D's proffered reason was not the true reason. P must actually prove that D intentionally discriminated.

**Comment.** In this type of case, D only has a burden of production, not of persuasion, although it will attempt to prove the factual basis of its proffered reason. In discrimination cases, courts usually speak of shifting burdens rather than presumptions.

---

## B.  CRIMINAL CASES

1.    **Burden of Persuasion.** In criminal cases, the guilt of the defendant must be proved beyond a reasonable doubt. This is a higher standard than either of the civil standards and is deemed necessary because of the seriousness of a criminal conviction. However, there are preliminary issues of a criminal case, such as lawfulness of a search, voluntariness of a confession, etc., which can be proved by a preponderance of the evidence.

## 2. Affirmative Defense--

---

**Patterson v. New York,** 432 U.S. 197 (1977).

---

**Facts.** After becoming estranged from his wife, Patterson (D) borrowed a rifle from an acquaintance and went to his father-in-law's home where he saw his wife through a window in a state of semiundress with her former fiancé. D entered the house and killed the former fiancé by shooting him twice in the head. D was charged with second degree murder. The two elements of the crime in New York were (i) intent to cause the death of another person, and (ii) causing the death of such person or another person. Malice aforethought is not an element of the crime. D raised the affirmative defense of acting under the influence of extreme emotional disturbance, which, if D proved by a preponderance of the evidence, would reduce the offense to manslaughter. The jury convicted D of murder. In the state courts, D unsuccessfully challenged the constitutionality of placing the burden of proof on him. D appeals.

**Issue.** May a state place the burden of proving the affirmative defense of extreme emotional disturbance upon the defendant when the crime with which he is charged does not include the element of malice aforethought?

**Held.** Yes. Judgment affirmed.

- ♦ In attempting to reverse his conviction in the court of appeals, D relied on *Mullaney v. Wilbur*, 421 U.S. 684 (1975). In *Mullaney*, the Court declared unconstitutional a Maine statute that required a defendant to rebut the statutory presumption that he committed the offense with "malice aforethought" by proving that he acted in the heat of passion on sudden provocation. This denied the defendant due process because the state is required to prove all elements of an offense to obtain a conviction.

- ♦ The difference between *Mullaney* and this case is that "malice aforethought" was an element of the crime in *Mullaney* and could not be supplied by a presumption. In this case, malice aforethought is not an element of the offense.

- ♦ The affirmative defense D asserts is an expanded version of the common law defense of heat of passion. The state does not need to recognize the defense; it may allocate the burden as it sees fit if it does allow the defense. Here, the burden was allocated to D by omitting malice from the elements of the crime.

**Dissent** (Powell, Brennan, Marshall, JJ.). The Court's holding allows a legislature to shift the burden of persuasion regarding any factor in a criminal case as long as the statute defining the crime is drafted to place the factor as an affirmative defense rather than as an element of the crime. This is too formalistic.

---

3. **Presumptions and Inferences.**

   a. **Introduction.** A crime is defined by a series of elements, each of which must be proved by the prosecution in order to result in a conviction. The courts have held that the prosecution cannot rely on presumptions to prove the case, although reasonable inferences are permitted.

   b. **Mandatory presumptions not permitted--**

---

## Sandstrom v. Montana, 442 U.S. 510 (1979).

---

**Facts.** Sandstrom (D) confessed to killing Annie Jessen. He was charged with "deliberate homicide" because he "purposely or knowingly caused the death of Annie Jessen." At trial, the defense argued that although D admitted to killing Jessen, he did not do so with the required intent. The intent was lacking due to D having a personality disorder that was aggravated by alcohol consumption. The trial court instructed the jury that "the law presumes that a person intends the ordinary consequences of his voluntary acts." D was convicted and sentenced to 100 years in prison. The state supreme court affirmed, and the United States Supreme Court granted certiorari.

**Issue.** When intent is an element of the crime charged, may the law presume that a person intends the ordinary consequences of his voluntary acts?

**Held.** No. Judgment reversed and case remanded.

♦ Because of the way in which the jury instruction was phrased, that "the law presumes that a person intends the ordinary consequences of his voluntary acts," the jury could have interpreted it in several ways. The jury could have interpreted the instruction as a permissive presumption, or one that only required D to come forward with "some" evidence in rebuttal. This would not be an unconstitutional interpretation.

♦ However, the jury also might have believed that the presumption was conclusive, or irrebuttable. Alternatively, the jury might have interpreted the instruction as a direction to find intent upon proof of D's voluntary actions unless D proved the contrary, thereby shifting the burden of persuasion to D on the element of intent. Either of these presumptions would unconstitutionally shift the burden of proof to D. Therefore, because D's jury may have interpreted the instruction in an unconstitutional manner, the conviction must be reversed.

---

   c. **Use of permissive presumptions--**

---

## County of Ulster v. Allen, 442 U.S. 140 (1979).

---

**Facts.** Under New York law, the presence of a firearm in a car is presumptive evidence of its illegal possession by all persons occupying the car. Allen, an adult male, was riding in a car with two other adult males and a 16-year-old girl. The car was stopped for speeding and the officer saw two large-caliber handguns in the girl's open hand-bag. The girl and the three adult males (Ds) were charged with illegal possession of handguns. At trial, the jury was instructed that it could infer illegal possession by all persons in the car upon proof that a firearm was present in the car. Ds were convicted. Allen and the two other adult males brought a federal habeas corpus proceeding, claiming that the use of the presumption was improper. The Second Circuit Court of Appeals held the state law unconstitutional. The Supreme Court granted certiorari.

**Issue.** May the prosecution use a permissive presumption to prove an element of a crime?

**Held.** Yes. Judgment reversed.

♦ A permissive presumption is one that a jury may reject even when not rebutted by the defense. Such a presumption does not shift the burden of proof. However, it can affect the "reasonable doubt" standard if, under the facts of the particular case, there is no rational way the jury could make the connection permitted by the inference. Such presumptions must be examined in light of the particular facts of each case.

♦ Here, the presumption of possession is rational. The handguns were large and obvious, and Ds were not casual passengers. The jury could infer that Ds attempted to conceal the guns in the girl's purse when the car was stopped for speeding.

♦ This case involved a permissive presumption, not a mandatory presumption. A permissive presumption need only satisfy the "more likely than not" standard rather than the reasonable doubt test because the presumption is not the only evidence upon which the prosecution relies to satisfy its burden.

♦ When a mandatory presumption (one which the jury must accept unless rebutted) is used, its validity is based on the presumption's accuracy in the run of cases. This is because the jury may not reject it based on its independent evaluation of the facts. Because a jury must accept such a presumption even if it is the sole evidence of an element of the offense, the case may not rest entirely on the presumption unless the fact proved is sufficient to support the inference of guilt beyond a reasonable doubt.

♦ Here, the presumption was permissive and satisfied the "more likely than not" standard.

**Dissent** (Powell, Brennan, Stewart, Marshall, JJ.). Under the presumption given in the instructions, the jury could have based its conclusion solely on its belief that Ds were in the car. Yet, the presumption is not "more likely than not" to be true. The existence of other evidence should not allow the jury to use a presumption that does not meet the basic test of the rational basis for a presumption.

---

# XI. JUDICIAL NOTICE

## A. INTRODUCTION

1. **Definition.** Judicial notice is the process whereby the trier of fact accepts certain facts as true without the necessity of formal proof. Thus, judicial notice is a substitute for evidence. Note that the judicial notice doctrine does not allow the trial judge or jury to substitute their personal knowledge for facts in the record.

2. **Legislative vs. Adjudicative Facts.** Most cases involving judicial notice concern adjudicative, not legislative, facts. When courts or commentators speak of judicial notice, they usually mean judicial notice of adjudicative facts. It is important to distinguish between the two.

## B. ADJUDICATIVE FACTS

1. **Definition.** Adjudicative facts are matters of consequence to the resolution of the factual issues in the particular case. These facts would be the subject of proof, except that, for one reason or another, judicial notice may be taken of them—usually because no reasonable person could dispute them. Under Rule 201(b), a judicially noticed fact must be one not subject to reasonable dispute in that it is either:

   a. Generally known within the territorial jurisdiction of the trial court; or

   b. Capable of accurate and ready determination by resort to sources whose accuracy cannot reasonably be questioned.

2. **Examples.** As stated, adjudicative facts are facts that are relevant to the case, but not disputable. Examples of adjudicative facts include: that the boiling point of water is 212° Fahrenheit; that the human body cannot survive immersion in molten lead; and, in an action for breach of contract to locate a purchaser of crude oil, that at the time of the alleged breach there was an Arab oil embargo and an increase in the price of oil.

3. **Procedure.** Judicial notice may be taken at any stage of the proceeding, including on appeal. A court has discretion to take judicial notice, whether requested by the parties or not. A court must take judicial notice if requested by a party and supplied with the necessary information. Also, a party is entitled to an opportunity to be heard regarding the propriety of the taking of judicial notice.

4. **Judge's Personal Belief--**

**Government of the Virgin Islands v. Gereau**, 523 F.2d 140 (3rd Cir. 1975).

**Facts.** After nine days of deliberations, a jury convicted Gereau and others (Ds) of first degree murder, first degree assault, and robbery. Two days later, Ds moved for a new trial, claiming the verdict had not been assented to by all the jurors. A juror testified that one of the jury attendants, Foye, asked how the deliberations were going and said that she wanted them to hurry up so she could go home. Foye denied having made the statement. The judge chose to believe Foye because he knew that she was grateful to earn extra income as a jury matron. The judge denied D's motion. D appeals.

**Issue.** May a judge rely on his personal, subjective belief about the needs and motives of a witness he knows personally in making a factual determination about credibility?

**Held.** No. Judgment affirmed on other grounds.

♦    The judge in this case was taking judicial notice of extra-record, adjudicative facts. To be the proper subject of judicial notice, a fact must be either a matter of common knowledge or capable of immediate and accurate determination by resort to easily accessible sources of indisputable accuracy.

♦    There is a clear line between a judge's personal knowledge as a private man and the matters of which he takes judicial notice as a judge. In this case, the judge's knowledge of Foye was personal knowledge and did not qualify for judicial notice.

♦    The juror who spoke to Foye did not say whether she was influenced by Foye's statement. However, she did vote guilty on all of the jury ballots. She also did not mention Foye's statement to any other jurors. Therefore, Foye's statement could not have affected the jury and there was no prejudice to D.

## C.  CRIMINAL CASES

1.    **Conclusiveness of Judicial Notice.** Rule 201(g) provides that in civil actions, the court must instruct the jury to accept as conclusive any fact judicially noticed. In criminal cases, however, the court must instruct the jury that it may, but is not required to, accept as conclusive any fact judicially noticed.

2.    **Judicial Notice on Appeal--**

**United States v. Jones**, 580 F.2d 219 (6th Cir. 1978).

**Facts.** Jones (D) was convicted by a jury of illegally intercepting telephone conversations. The statute required that the phone used be furnished by a common carrier. The prosecution showed that the phone D used was furnished by South Central Bell Telephone Company, but offered no evidence that South Central was a common carrier. After considering D's argument that the government failed to prove the intercepted wire communication was from a common carrier's line, the judge entered a judgment of acquittal. The prosecution appeals.

**Issue.** In a criminal case, may facts be judicially noticed at the appellate stage?

**Held.** No. Judgment affirmed.

♦ The fact that South Central was a common carrier could have been judicially noticed, but no request for such notice was made. The note to Federal Rule 201(f) indicates that judicial notice may be taken at trial or on appeal, but the difference between civil and criminal trials changes this rule.

♦ Under Federal Rule 201(g), a jury need not accept as conclusive facts judicially noticed by the court in criminal trials. If judicial notice at the appellate stage of criminal cases were allowed, the jury would not have a chance to pass on the noticed fact, in violation of Rule 201(g).

---

## D. LEGISLATIVE FACTS

1.  **Definition.** Legislative facts are those facts that are relevant to legal reasoning and the law-making process.

    a.  **Examples.** Some examples of legislative facts include: that racially separate schools are inherently unequal; that women have at times been the object of invidious legislative and judicial discrimination; that electronic methods exist which, without physical entry, can intrude upon the privacy of citizens; and that Congress enacted the National Labor Relations Act to redress what it felt was the imbalance in the bargaining power of the employer as against the worker.

    b.  **Applicable law.** Legislative facts also include the applicable law, statutes, judicial decisions, etc., without which legal issues cannot be decided. Some jurisdictions require that courts take judicial notice of federal and state law and rules of procedure, as well as English language definitions and meanings. Courts commonly take judicial notice of the laws of other states and nations and administrative regulations and orders.

    c.  **Scarcity of case law.** Although a court must take judicial notice of legislative facts in virtually every case in which it makes a decision based upon policy or draws a legal conclusion, there are very few rules governing this type of judicial notice. Most courts simply take judicial notice of legislative facts without any reference to the fact that they are doing so.

2.   **Judicial Notice of General Knowledge.** In *Muller v. Oregon*, 208 U.S. 412 (1907), the Court addressed the constitutionality of an Oregon statute that limited to 10 the maximum number of hours women can work in laundries and factories. The Court found a rational basis for the statute, partly because of a widespread belief that the female physical structure justified special legislative protection of women's working conditions. The Court took judicial cognizance of this matter of general knowledge, based on a widespread and long continued belief concerning the issue.

3.   **Judicial Notice in Constitutional Challenge--**

## Houser v. State, 540 P.2d 412 (Wash. 1975).

**Facts.** Houser (P) brought a class action suit against the state of Washington (D), claiming the law establishing a minimum age of 21 for drinking alcohol was unconstitutional. To determine whether there was a rational relationship between the drinking age law and a legitimate state purpose, the court took judicial notice of studies submitted by D. The trial court granted summary judgment for D. P claimed the studies did not qualify for judicial notice because the facts they contained were not well established and authoritatively settled. P appeals.

**Issue.** May a court take judicial notice of legislative facts when considering a constitutional challenge to a statute?

**Held.** Yes. Judgment affirmed.

♦   The court was not required to inquire into the facts of the particular case, but instead had to examine the general relationship between the attainment of age 21 and the effect of alcohol consumption. It was a legal, not a factual, determination whether there was a rational relationship between the statutory distinction and the state purposes it was alleged to serve.

♦   The court's finding that it was rational to believe that the discrimination corresponded to a permissible state objective was a step in the court's legal reasoning, not a finding of fact. The rules that restrict judicial notice are not applicable to fact findings that simply supply premises in the process of legal reasoning. Reputable scientific studies are a proper source of information to use in assessing the existence of this type of rational relationship.

# E. CLASSIFICATION

1. **Introduction.** Article II of the Federal Rules which contains the rules on judicial notice applies only to judicial notice of adjudicative facts. Consequently, the outcome of a challenge to judicial notice can depend on the classification of the facts noticed.

2. **Judicial Notice of Legislative Fact in Criminal Trial--**

---

**United States v. Gould,** 536 F.2d 216 (8th Cir. 1976).

---

**Facts.** Gould and Carey (Ds) were convicted of conspiring to import and importing cocaine under the Controlled Substances Import and Export Act. At trial, the jury was instructed that cocaine hydrochloride is a Schedule II controlled substance, with no foundation having been laid as to what substances are within Schedule II. (Schedule II is part of the federal statute that lists controlled substances and includes coca leaves and any derivative thereof.) There was evidence at trial that the substance D imported was cocaine hydrochloride, but not that it was a derivative of coca leaves. D appeals.

**Issue.** Is a jury bound by judicial notice of a legislative fact in a criminal case?

**Held.** Yes. Judgment affirmed.

♦ Although the fact that cocaine hydrochloride is derived from coca leaves may not be common knowledge, it is capable of certain and easy verification. It is a proper subject of judicial notice.

♦ Federal Rule 201(g) states that a jury is not required to accept as conclusive any fact judicially noticed in a criminal case. However, this rule applies only to adjudicative facts. The fact noticed in this case was legislative because it is an established truth that applies universally and does not vary from case to case. Courts often have to judicially notice legislative facts in order to discern the applicable law. In such cases, the fact noticed is binding on the jury as a statement of the law.

♦ The jury exercised its fact-finding function when it determined that the confiscated substance was cocaine hydrochloride. The law classified that substance as a Schedule II controlled substance.

**Comment.** Courts sometimes take judicial notice of facts that have come to light after the legislation involved was adopted. For example, in *Roe v. Wade,* 410 U.S. 113 (1973), the Supreme Court took notice of modern medical developments that reduced the dangers present when the abortion statutes were originally adopted. The reduced risk was a major factor in the decision because it minimized the state interests competing with the right of privacy.

---

# XII. PRIVILEGES

## A. SCOPE AND EFFECT OF EVIDENTIARY PRIVILEGES

1. **Introduction.** Most rules of evidence (such as the hearsay rule, opinion rule, etc.) are designed to keep prejudicial information from being presented to the trier of fact. Privileges, however, do not have this purpose—they are designed to exclude helpful evidence in situations where it is considered more important to keep certain information confidential than to require disclosure of all information relevant to deciding the issues in the case. Because privileges have the effect of protecting what otherwise would be useful evidence, most jurisdictions provide that the only recognized privileges are those provided by statute. [*See, e.g.,* Cal. Evid. Code §911] Article V of the Federal Rules of Procedure simply provides that the law of privileges is governed by the common law, except that federal courts must look to state rules of privilege in diversity cases. The rationale for this position is that a witness's ability to testify may often affect the outcome of the case and therefore should be governed by state law whenever state law otherwise provides the rule of decision. The rule thus prevents "forum shopping" between the federal and state courts.

2. **General Principles Applicable to All Privileges.**

   a. **Who may assert privilege—in general.** A privilege is personal in nature; *i.e.,* it can be claimed only by the "holder"—the person whose interest or relationship is sought to be protected (*e.g.,* spouse, patient, client, etc.). If the privilege is held by two or more persons, each of them may claim the privilege.

      1) A privilege also may be asserted by a person authorized to do so on behalf of the holder.

         a) For example, if the holder is legally incompetent, the guardian can assert (or waive) the privilege.

         b) Similarly, because privileges generally "survive" the death of the holder, they can be asserted (or waived) by the holder's executor or administrator. There are some exceptions, however; *e.g.,* the privilege to withhold confidential communications between spouses terminates in many states on the death of either spouse.

         c) In addition, the person with whom the confidence was shared may, in certain cases, claim the privilege on behalf of the holder (*e.g.,* an attorney is authorized to assert the client's privilege in the latter's absence).

2) Although a privilege is personal, if neither the holder of the privilege nor anyone entitled to assert it for her is present when the testimony is sought to be introduced, then the court on its own motion, or the motion of any party, must exclude the testimony which is subject to the claim of privilege. [Cal. Evid. Code §916]

b. **Requirement of confidentiality; presumption.** When a communication is claimed to be privileged, it must always be shown that it was made in confidence. Note, however, that many states recognize a presumption that disclosures made in the course of a privileged relationship (*i.e.,* between spouses, attorney-client, etc.) were made in confidence. [*See, e.g.,* Cal. Evid. Code §917]

c. **Waiver of privilege.**

1) **By failure to object.** As with other exclusionary rules of evidence, privileges are deemed waived if not raised by appropriate and timely objection when the testimony is first offered. The objection must be specific; the general objection "incompetent, irrelevant, and immaterial" will not suffice.

2) **By consent.** Moreover, any person entitled to claim a privilege may waive it by consent. Such consent may be manifested by:

a) Failure to claim the privilege when the holder has the legal standing and opportunity to claim the privilege;

b) Contractual provision waiving in advance the right to claim the privilege; or

c) Voluntary disclosure by the holder (or by another if with holder's consent) of all or a significant part of the privileged matter, except when the disclosure is itself privileged—*e.g.,* D tells her priest what she previously told her attorney. [*See* Cal. Evid. Code §912]

3) **Distinguish—situations that do not constitute waiver.**

a) **Error.** There is no waiver of privilege if the disclosure was compelled erroneously or made without opportunity for the holder to claim the privilege. Hence, evidence obtained in an earlier trial or proceeding in which the witness's claim of privilege was erroneously denied cannot be used in a later trial. [Cal. Evid. Code §919]

b) **Joint privilege.** When a privilege is held jointly (*e.g.,* two persons consult a lawyer together), a waiver of the privilege by one holder does not affect the right of the other to claim the privilege. [Cal. Evid. Code §912(c)]

### d. Effect of eavesdroppers.

**1) Traditional view.** The prevailing view is that an eavesdropper can testify to what he has overheard, regardless of whether his overhearing was due to the carelessness of the communicating parties. Some courts rationalize this on the theory that the holder was responsible to take precautions to safeguard the confidentiality of the communications and therefore must be deemed to have "waived" the privilege.

**2) Modern trend.** A significant number of modern cases and statutes assert that as long as the holder of the privilege was not negligent (*i.e.,* no reasonable basis to believe that the communication would be overheard), there is no "waiver" of the privilege and hence the eavesdropper is not permitted to testify. [*See, e.g.,* Cal. Evid. Code §954]

### e. Constitutional limitations on claim of privilege. In a criminal case, a claim of privilege may be denied if its exercise would deprive the accused of her right to present her defense.

## B. ATTORNEY-CLIENT PRIVLEGE

**1. Basic Rule.** A client of an attorney has a privilege to refuse to disclose, and to prevent the attorney or anyone else from disclosing, any confidential communication made between the client and the attorney related to the rendering of legal services. The oldest privilege recognized at common law, the attorney-client privilege is intended to encourage full disclosure by the client to the attorney to facilitate proper legal counsel. The privilege belongs to the client; only the client can waive the privilege. To be protected, a communication must have the characteristics enumerated below.

**a. Attorney.** The communication must have been made to a member of the Bar, or to an employee for transmission to the attorney. Actual employment of the attorney is not required; communications are protected even if the attorney does not accept the case or the client does not hire the attorney.

**b. Client.** The client who communicates to the attorney may be a natural person, a corporation, or any similar entity. *See* the special rules for corporate clients discussed *infra*.

**c. Legal advice.** The privilege does not apply if the client was consulting the attorney for business advice instead of legal advice.

**2. Communication.** To be protected, communication between the client and attorney must have been intended to convey a specific meaning. Such communications include discussions made by the client to the attorney, as well as the attorney's legal opinion and advice to the client based thereon.

    a.    **Attorney's observations.** Normally, the attorney's observations of the client's condition, the identity of the client, the amount of fees and payments thereof, and the fact that a consultation took place are not privileged, although there are exceptions.

    b.    **Documents.** Documents provided by the client to the attorney are not privileged unless prepared specifically to give the attorney information. Documents prepared by the attorney are not protected by the attorney-client privilege, but are protected by the work-product doctrine discussed in *Upjohn Co. v. United States, infra.*

    c.    **Attorney's investigation--**

---

## People v. Meredith, 631 P.2d 46 (Cal. 1981).

**Facts.** Wade and Otis entered a club one night. Scott stayed outside. Meredith (D) arrived and told Scott he was going to rob Wade. D asked Scott to go in and ask Otis (who was a friend of D and Scott) to bring Wade out to Wade's car. When Wade and Otis went to the car, D attacked Wade. After a brief struggle, two shots were fired. Wade fell, and D ran away. Scott told his lawyer, Schenk, that he had seen a wallet on the ground near Wade when he fell and that he put it in a bag with beer that Wade and Otis had purchased earlier in the evening and had left by the car, and he eventually took the bag home. He found $100 in the wallet and divided it with D. After trying unsuccessfully to burn the wallet, Scott threw it in a burn barrel behind his house. Schenk retained an investigator who found the wallet and brought it to Schenk. Inside, Schenk found credit cards with Wade's name on them. He turned the wallet over to a detective. D and Scott were charged with first degree murder and robbery of Wade. At a preliminary hearing, the prosecution called Schenk and his investigator. The court ordered Schenk to say whether his contact with Scott led to the discovery of the wallet, and Schenk said "yes." The investigator then testified that he had found the wallet in a garbage can behind Scott's residence. The investigator repeated this testimony at trial. D and Scott were convicted. Scott's conviction was based on his being a co-conspirator with D. Scott appeals, claiming that the location of the wallet was a privileged communication.

**Issue.** If a criminal defense lawyer finds physical evidence based on his client's privileged communication and then removes that evidence, must the lawyer reveal where he found the evidence when he turns it over to the prosecution?

**Held.** Yes. Judgment affirmed.

    ♦    When Scott told Schenk where the wallet was located, this was a privileged communication. The privilege was not waived when Schenk told the investigator because this disclosure was reasonably necessary to accomplish the purpose for which Schenk had been consulted.

- Once he recovered the wallet, Schenk had a duty to turn it over to the prosecution. In *State v. Olwell*, 394 P.2d 681 (Wash. 1964), the court held that if the securing of physical evidence is the direct result of information given to the lawyer by the client, the lawyer must turn the evidence over but should not reveal the source of the evidence.

- If a defense lawyer alters or removes physical evidence, he deprives the prosecution of the chance to see the evidence in its original condition or location. The best way to balance the competing interests is to require the defense lawyer who removes or alters evidence to reveal the original location or condition of the evidence. If the lawyer chooses to leave the evidence in its original condition, his observations are protected.

**Comment.** A lawyer who conceals or destroys evidence can be prosecuted or have his license suspended.

---

3. **Confidentiality Requirement.** The communication must have been made outside the presence of strangers under circumstances that show that the parties intended the communication to be confidential.

   a. **Presumption.** Many states have a statutory presumption that any communication between a client and an attorney was made in confidence.

   b. **Authorized third parties.** If third parties who are *reasonably necessary* to the consultation are present at the consultation, the privilege is not lost. These third parties may include relatives, business associates, or joint clients.

   c. **Use of agents.** If communications are made to agents out of the reasonable necessity of transmitting information between the attorney and client, they are protected. Common examples of such agents include secretaries, messengers, and foreign language interpreters.

      1) **Co-defendant's counsel.** Communications to the counsel of a co-plaintiff or co-defendant are likewise protected.

      2) **Physician.** If an attorney hires a physician to examine the client, the physician's report is not privileged under the physician-patient privilege because no treatment is contemplated. However, the attorney-client privilege will apply if the examination is necessary to allow the client to communicate her condition to the attorney. The physician acts as the client's agent in communicating with the attorney.

> **3)    Other professionals.** If information is transmitted to an attorney by the client's accountant or tax advisor, it may be protected by the attorney-client privilege.
>
> > **a)    Accountant hired by law firm--**

---

# United States v. Kovel, 296 F.2d 918 (2nd Cir. 1961).

---

**Facts.** Kovel (D) was a former IRS agent and accounting specialist. He worked for Kamerman & Kamerman, a law firm specializing in tax law. D was subpoenaed to testify to a grand jury about one of the firm's clients who was being investigated for income tax violations. The firm told the prosecutor that the attorney-client privilege applied because D was an employee supervised by the partners, and D could not disclose privileged communications without the client's consent. The prosecutor disagreed based on the fact that D was not an attorney. When D refused to answer questions, claiming privilege, he was sentenced for criminal contempt. D appeals.

**Issue.** Does the attorney-client privilege extend to accountants whose presence during confidential communications between an attorney and client is necessary to assist the attorney in rendering legal advice to the client?

**Held.** Yes. Judgment vacated and remanded.

- ♦ The traditional rule extended the privilege to nonlawyer employees who had menial or ministerial responsibilities. In modern times, however, lawyers require the assistance of more specialized employees, including accountants, to handle the complex legal and factual issues that can arise in a case.

- ♦ By analogy, a lawyer whose client speaks a foreign language has several options. He can: (i) send the client to an interpreter to record and translate the client's story, (ii) have a nonlawyer employee act as an interpreter in the lawyer's presence, or (iii) have the client bring an interpreter to the interview with the lawyer. In each case, the privilege would extend to the communication with the interpreter.

- ♦ Accounting concepts can be as foreign as an unknown language, and lawyers may require the assistance of a nonlawyer accountant employee to handle cases. There is no privilege for accountant-client communications per se. However, the attorney-client privilege protects a client's communications made in confidence for the purpose of obtaining legal advice from a lawyer, even if an accountant is present.

- ♦ If the client goes to the lawyer, who then brings an accountant into the interview, the privilege prevents the accountant from disclosing the communications. If the client goes to an accountant first, and then to a lawyer, the communication with the accountant is not privileged.

---

### d.    Eavesdroppers--

## Suburban Sew 'N Sweep v. Swiss-Bernia, 91 F.R.D. 254 (N.D. Ill. 1981).

**Facts.** Surburban Sew 'N Sweep and other sewing machine retailers (Ps) sued Swiss-Bernia (D) and other manufacturers claiming price discrimination and conspiracy under the antitrust acts. To build their case, Ps searched a dumpster in a parking lot of an office building occupied by D. Among other things, Ps found drafts of letters from D's president to D's lawyer that contained confidential information. Ps used information in the letters in its interrogatories. The magistrate declined to compel discovery on the ground that Ps improperly obtained the letters. Ps appeal.

**Issue.** Does the attorney-client privilege extend to otherwise confidential correspondence that the client puts in the trash?

**Held.** No. Judgment reversed.

♦    Traditionally, the parties to a privileged communication had nearly absolute responsibility to maintain confidentiality. The development of sophisticated eavesdropping devices has led to a modification of this rule. The privilege now extends to prevent disclosure of a privileged communication where the communication has been involuntarily disclosed, such as where a confidential document is stolen.

♦    At the same time, clients remain responsible in insuring confidentiality to the extent possible. The privilege does not extend to cases where information is transmitted in public or otherwise not adequately safeguarded.

♦    The key is whether the client intended to maintain the confidentiality of the documents, as shown by the precautions taken. In determining whether the precautions were adequate, the courts should consider: (i) the effect on uninhibited attorney-client consultation of not allowing the privilege under the circumstances, and (ii) the ability of the parties to protect against the disclosure.

♦    In this case, Ds simply put the letters in the trash. This is not sufficient precaution to protect the communication. Ds could have destroyed the documents or made them illegible before putting them in the trash.

**Comment.** Property put in the trash is not protected by the Fourth Amendment, which protects against searches by government agents.

---

### 4.    Corporate Clients.

#### a.    Statements of corporate officials and employees. An employee's communications with the corporation's counsel are protected by the

corporation's privilege, not the employee's, when the employee acts in a representative capacity. If an employee gives an ordinary witness statement, which is not required by his job, to the corporate attorney, the statement is not privileged. Traditionally, only statements by high corporate officials were protected by the privilege, but this rule has been relaxed.

b.  **Work-product doctrine and corporate attorney-client privilege--**

---

## Upjohn Co. v. United States, 449 U.S. 383 (1981).

---

**Facts.** Upjohn Co. (D), a multinational corporation, discovered that one of its foreign subsidiaries had apparently bribed foreign government officials to secure government business. As part of an internal investigation, D's attorneys sent questionnaires to its foreign managers and conducted interviews with these people and certain other employees. The IRS initiated an investigation of the tax consequences and issued a summons for production of the questionnaires and interview notes. D refused to produce the documents, claiming attorney-client privilege and work-product doctrine protection. The lower courts ordered production and D appeals.

**Issue.** Are disclosures made by corporate employees to corporate attorneys within the attorney-client privilege?

**Held.** Yes. Judgment reversed.

♦  The lower courts held that the attorney-client privilege applies only to communications made by employees responsible for directing D's actions, in response to legal advice. This "control group" test is too restrictive because employees at any level could, acting within the scope of their employment, cause serious legal problems for D. D's attorneys also would need to obtain information from these employees to formulate appropriate advice.

♦  To the extent the requested documents were not communications from the client and thus privileged, the documents were attorney work product. Documents that reveal the attorneys' mental processes in evaluating the information are privileged under the work-product doctrine. [*See* Fed. R. Civ. P. 26]

**Concurrence** (Burger, C.J.). The Court should adopt a specific rule about the privilege, whereby all communications between an employee or former employee and an attorney authorized by management are privileged.

**Comment.** The only protections applicable in the corporate setting are the two involved in this case. In *Upjohn,* the Court broadened the application of the attorney-client privilege in the corporate context, but the work-product doctrine still provides only limited protection.

---

**5.** **Exceptions to Coverage.** The normal limits on privilege may be disregarded where a disclosure would defeat the overall policy purposes of the privilege.

**a.** **Client identity--**

---

## *In Re* Grand Jury Investigation 83-2-35 (Durant), 723 F.2d 447 (6th Cir. 1983).

---

**Facts.** The FBI traced a number of checks stolen from IBM to various banking accounts. A check drawn on one of these accounts was made payable to the law firm of Durant (D). When the FBI inquired, D admitted that he had received the check for $15,000 in payment for services rendered to a client in two cases. D refused to disclose the identity of the client, asserting the attorney-client privilege. D was subpoenaed to appear before the grand jury. He refused to identify his client. The government sought an order compelling D to disclose the client. The court held D in contempt for refusing to reveal the client's name. The government also sought to compel D to provide a list of all of his clients. D appeals from the contempt finding and moves to quash the subpoena of his client list.

**Issue.** Was the identity of D's client protected by the attorney-client privilege?

**Held.** No. Judgment affirmed and motion denied.

♦ The general rule provides that a client's identity is not within the protection of the privilege. There are exceptions to this rule, as set forth in *Baird v. Koerner*, 279 F.2d 623 (9th Cir. 1960). In that case, a lawyer made a tax payment on behalf of an undisclosed taxpayer. The court recognized an exception that applies when the circumstances are such that the name of the client is material only to show an acknowledgment of guilt on the part of the client of the very offenses for which the lawyer was engaged. This is called the "legal advice" exception.

♦ Another exception exists where disclosure of the client's identity would be tantamount to disclosing an otherwise privileged communication. This situation arises when so much of the actual communication has already been disclosed, by the lawyer or by independent sources, that identification of the client, or of fees paid, would amount to disclosure of a confidential communication. This is the "confidential communications" exception.

♦ A third exception arises when disclosure of the client's identity would provide the "last link" of an existing chain of incriminating evidence that likely would lead to the client's indictment. This exception should not be recognized, however, because it does not focus on preserving the confidentiality of communications.

♦ In this case, D justified his refusal to disclose the client's identity on the ground that disclose might implicate the client in criminal activity. This justification is unrelated to confidentiality or communication, so it cannot be accepted. The threat of arrest is not a legitimate ground for D's refusal, because it relies on the "last link" theory, which is not a valid exception.

♦ D also claimed that the "legal advice" exception applies to this case. To rely on this exception, D would have to show that a strong possibility existed that disclosure would implicate the client in the very matter for which the client came to him. D has the burden of proof on this matter. However, D did not seek an in camera ex parte hearing with the judge to explain how the legal advice exception applies to this case. He merely made an unsupported assertion, which is insufficient to demonstrate a strong possibility.

**Comment.** Several courts, including the Ninth Circuit, now hold that only the "confidential communications" exception is valid.

---

b. **Future crime or fraud--**

## State v. Phelps, 454 P.2d 901 (Or. Ct. App. 1976).

**Facts.** Phelps (D) was charged with DUI. He told his lawyer that he had several witnesses who would testify that D was not driving. D's lawyer investigated and concluded that D was lying. When confronted, D admitted that he had lied about who was driving. D promised not to use perjured testimony in the case, and D's lawyer withdrew. D later retained another lawyer and used the perjured testimony to successfully defend the charge. D's first lawyer was called before a grand jury, where he testified about his conversations with D regarding the contemplated perjury. D was indicted for perjury and witness tampering. At a hearing, the court held that D's first lawyer could not be compelled to testify about privileged communications unless D waived the privilege. The state (P) appeals.

**Issue.** Does a client's plan to use perjured testimony in his defense fall within the future crime exception to the rule of privilege?

**Held.** Yes. Judgment reversed and case remanded.

♦ The testimony that P seeks concerns D's use of perjured testimony in his trial. This was a crime that was future at the time of D's discussion with his first lawyer. The privilege does not protect discussion of future crime or fraud intended to conceal past wrongdoing.

♦ D claims that the future crime or fraud exception should not apply where the crime could not be prevented by disclosure because it had already been committed by the time of trial, even though it had not been committed at the time of the communication. However, crime prevention is not the only purpose for the rule.

♦ Advice regarding future crimes would not be professional services but conspiracy. The privilege does not extend to conspiracy. Once the communication pertains to a future crime, it is simply not privileged, whether or not the client commits the crime before the lawyer reveals the client's intention.

---

## C. PSYCHOTHERAPIST-PATIENT PRIVILEGE

1.  **Introduction.** Although not recognized at common law, a statutory physician-patient privilege has been widely adopted to encourage full disclosure by patients so they may be effectively treated. The privilege belongs to the patient only and is normally permitted only in civil actions. The privilege usually extends to tests and diagnoses as well as to the patient's communications.

2.  **Psychotherapist-Patient Privilege.** The physician-patient privilege has been extended in a few states to patients of psychotherapists, on the rationale that full disclosure between doctor and patient is even more necessary for the treatment of mental and emotional illness. [Cal. Evid. Code §1010] The rule is that a patient can refuse to disclose confidential communications between himself and his psychotherapist made for the purpose of diagnosing or treating his mental or emotional condition. He can also prevent testimony by the psychotherapist or by any person participating in such diagnosis or treatment under the psychotherapist's direction, *e.g.*, members of the patient's family or possibly members of therapy groups. [Cal. Evid. Code §1014] This privilege is somewhat broader than the normal physician-patient privilege.

    a.  **Scope of rule.**

        1)  The privilege applies to any litigation—civil or criminal, whereas the physician-patient privilege is generally recognized only in civil proceedings. It applies whether or not the patient is a party to such proceedings.

        2)  The privilege belongs to the patient, not to the psychotherapist. However, if the patient is absent, the psychotherapist can assert it on his behalf. [Cal. Evid. Code §1015]

        3)  The "psychotherapist" need not be a licensed physician; the privilege applies to certified psychologists as well. [Cal. Evid. Code §1010]

    b.  **Exceptions.** Because the psychotherapist privilege is broader than the physician privilege, fewer exceptions are recognized:

1) **Commitment proceedings against patient.** If the psychotherapist has determined that the patient is in need of hospitalization for mental illness, she may testify. California Evidence Code section 1024 limits this exception to situations where the patient is violent.

2) **Court-ordered examinations.** Communications by the patient in the course of a court-ordered mental examination are not privileged.

3) **Mental condition in issue.** Whenever the patient (or his estate) has placed his mental condition in issue, *e.g.*, by claiming insanity as a defense in a criminal case, he (or his estate) cannot assert the privilege. [Cal. Evid. Code §1016]

3. **Social Workers--**

---

**Jaffee v. Redmond,** 518 U.S. 1 (1996).

---

**Facts.** Redmond (D), a former police officer, and her employer were sued after she shot and killed Allen while on patrol duty. D believed that Allen was about to stab a man he had been chasing with a butcher knife. Jaffee (P), administrator of Allen's estate, presented testimony at trial that directly contradicted D's version of the incident. After learning through discovery that D had had about 50 counseling sessions with Beyer, a social worker, after the shooting, P moved for access to Beyer's notes. D asserted a psychotherapist-patient privilege. The court granted P access. Neither D nor Beyer complied, and both either refused to answer questions regarding their conversations or claimed that they did not recall the details. The judge instructed the jury that the refusal to turn over the notes had no legal justification and that the jury could presume the notes would have been unfavorable to D. The jury found for P. The court of appeals reversed and remanded for a new trial, holding that "reason and experience" compelled recognition of a psychotherapist-patient privilege. The appeals court also held that the privilege would not apply if the evidentiary need for disclosure of the contents of the patient's counseling session outweighed the patient's privacy interests. The Supreme Court granted certiorari.

**Issue.** Should the federal courts recognize a psychotherapist-patient privilege against disclosure of confidential communications?

**Held.** Yes. Judgment affirmed.

♦ Rule 501 authorizes federal courts to define new privileges by interpreting common law principles in light of reason and experience.

♦ The privilege is rooted in the imperative need for confidence, trust, and the development of a confidential relationship between a psychotherapist and her patient. The privilege also serves the public interest "by facilitating the provision of appropriate treatment for individuals suffering the effects of a mental or emotional problem."

♦ The likely evidentiary benefit that would result if the privilege were denied is modest. Denial of the privilege would chill confidential communications between client and therapist, especially where litigation is likely, so the sought-after evidence would remain unspoken and would serve no greater truth-seeking function than if it were spoken and privileged.

♦ All 50 states and the District of Columbia have enacted into law some form of psychotherapist privilege. Without a corresponding federal privilege, the purpose of the state legislature to ensure confidential communications would be frustrated, as statements privileged in state court could still be admissible in federal court. The privilege was also recommended by the Advisory Committee.

♦ Social workers provide a significant amount of mental health treatment, particularly for the poor and for those of modest means. The federal privilege should be extended to communications made to licensed social workers in the course of psychotherapy.

♦ The balancing component adopted by the court of appeals would undermine the privilege and cannot be upheld. Making the confidentiality contingent on a trial judge's evaluation would eviscerate the effectiveness of the privilege. An uncertain privilege is little better than no privilege at all.

**Dissenting** (Scalia, J., Rehnquist, C.J.). This privilege is new, vast, and ill-defined in its scope. To characterize this privilege as analogous to the attorney-client privilege is incorrect. The attorney-client privilege is identified by the professional status of the person, not by the broad area of advice-giving practice by the person. Thus, although it seems a long step from attorney-client privilege to tax advisor-client or accountant-client privilege, it would be a shorter step if the attorney-client privilege were characterized as "legal advisor" privilege. The Court mentions the similarities between psychiatrists, psychologists, and social workers, but it does not mention the differences. The psychologist and psychiatrist are experts in psychotherapy; the social worker does not have this high degree of skill. It is not clear that the social worker degree even requires a course in psychotherapy. Because of this privilege, the federal courts will sometimes be tools of injustice rather than finders of truth.

---

## D. SPOUSAL PRIVILEGES

1. **Introduction.** There are two separate privileges based on the marital relationship: (i) the privilege not to testify against one's spouse (or the privilege against adverse spousal testimony), and (ii) the privilege against revealing confidential communications.

## 2. Testimonial Privilege.

a. **Common law.** At common law, spouses were considered one legal entity, and since a party could not testify, neither spouse could testify for or against the other.

b. **Modern law.** Most states allow spouses to testify on behalf of the other in both civil and criminal proceedings. In civil cases, a spouse may be compelled to testify against the other. In criminal cases, the witness spouse may not be compelled to testify against the defendant spouse, but the defendant may not unilaterally prevent such testimony.

c. **Scope.** The privilege applies to all testimony against one's spouse and extends even to any record of the witness spouse's testimony given in an unprivileged proceeding. Thus, compelled spousal testimony in a civil case may not be used in a criminal case. The privilege may only be asserted during the marriage. Once divorced, the former spouses may be compelled to testify about matters that occurred during the marriage. In most states, an accused may avoid conviction by marrying the witness so she cannot be compelled to testify.

d. **Exceptions.** In some situations, the marriage is probably past saving, and the privilege therefore does not apply:

1) Crimes against the person or property of the other spouse;

2) Crimes against the children of either spouse; and

3) Statutory offenses against women (*e.g.*, the Mann Act and prostitution).

e. **Restricted to testifying spouse--**

---

## Trammel v. United States, 445 U.S. 40 (1980).

---

**Facts.** Trammel (D), his wife, and others worked together in smuggling and distributing illegal drugs. On one trip into the United States, D's wife was caught with four ounces of heroin. She agreed to testify against D and the others. Prior to trial, D moved for severance of his case on the ground that he planned to claim his privilege to prevent her from testifying against him. D's motion was denied and his wife was permitted to testify as to everything she had seen or heard during the marriage (except for confidential communications between herself and D). D was convicted and appealed. The court of appeals affirmed, and the Supreme Court granted certiorari.

**Issue.** May an accused invoke the privilege against adverse spousal testimony to exclude his wife's voluntary testimony?

**Held.** No. Judgment affirmed.

♦ The common law rationale for the privilege was based on the concept that a husband and wife were one and that the woman had no separate legal existence. Although this idea has been discarded, the privilege has continued due to its role in fostering the harmony and sanctity of the marital relationship. Unitl now, such testimony was admissible only if both spouses consented.

♦ The states, which primarily govern marriage and domestic relations, have tended to divest the accused of the privilege to bar spousal testimony. This trend is proper because the contemporary justification for the privilege is unpersuasive. If the testifying spouse wants to testify against the accused, their relationship probably lacks any harmony for the law to protect. The accused should not have the unilateral right to prevent the other spouse from accepting offers of leniency.

♦ The privilege therefore is restricted to the testifying spouse, who cannot be compelled to testify, but who cannot be prevented from testifying if she so desires.

**Comment.** Remember that this privilege is independent of the confidential communications between spouses privilege.

---

3. **Spousal Confidences Privilege.**

   a. **Introduction.** Separate from the privilege not to testify against one's spouse, there is a common law privilege that prevents disclosure of confidential communications between spouses made during their marriage. The privilege continues after termination of the marriage and may be asserted by either spouse, in any action, civil or criminal. The exceptions are the same as those for the other marital privilege, *i.e.*, no privilege for crimes against a spouse or child.

   b. **Privilege limited to communications--**

---

**United States v. Estes**, 793 F.2d 465 (2nd Cir. 1986).

---

**Facts.** Estes (D) worked for Purolator as a driver and guard of an armored car. One day he came home with a saddlebag full of cash. When his wife Lydia asked what was wrong, he poured the money onto their bed and told her that he had stolen the money from Purolator. Lydia hid $15,000 below their stairs, and D hid the rest outside. The couple started spending the money. D and Lydia were subsequently divorced. After a while, Lydia contacted the FBI and obtained a grant of immunity. She then taped conversations with D. D was charged with bank robbery and perjury. Lydia testified against him in detail. D was convicted of perjury. D appeals.

**Issue.** May a former spouse testify about her ex-husband's criminal act that took place during the marriage if her husband disclosed the act to her after it was completed?

**Held.** No. Judgment reversed and case remanded.

♦ Confidential marital communications are not protected by the spousal privilege if they concern ongoing criminal activity. D's theft was completed, rather than ongoing, when D told Lydia about it. This testimony should not have been admitted, and this was the most incriminating part of Lydia's testimony.

♦ The spousal privilege covers only communications, not acts, except in rare cases where the conduct is intended to convey a confidential message. Lydia could properly testify about the counting, hiding, and laundering of the cash that she observed and participated in. She could also testify about communications that were made in furtherance of unlawful joint criminal activity. This is the so-called "partnership in crime" exception to the spousal privilege.

---

## E. PRIVILEGE AGAINST SELF-INCRIMINATION

1. **Introduction.** The Fifth Amendment to the Constitution provides that no one can be compelled in a criminal case to be a witness against himself. This is the only testimonial privilege contained in the Constitution. The privilege was extended to the states as part of the Due Process Clause in the Fourteenth Amendment in *Malloy v. Hogan*, 378 U.S. 1 (1964). It has been applied to civil cases as well as criminal cases.

2. **Persons Protected.** The self-incrimination privilege belongs only to individuals, not to partnerships, corporations, or other entities. Thus, a corporate officer must produce corporate records, even if they would incriminate him personally.

3. **Waiver.** A criminal defendant waives the privilege by taking the stand, whereas any other witness waives it only by giving her first incriminating answer without objection. A criminal defendant does not waive her privilege:

   a. At her present trial by having waived it at a previous trial of the same charge;

   b. At trial by testifying about a threshold issue, such as the admissibility of a confession or of real evidence obtained by a challenged search; or

c. According to a greater number of courts, as to crimes unrelated to the one for which she is on trial and for which she has waived her privilege.

## 4. Adverse Inferences--

---

# Griffin v. California, 380 U.S. 609 (1965).

---

**Facts.** Griffin (D) was tried for first degree murder and refused to testify on his own behalf. As permitted by the California Constitution, the prosecutor commented on D's refusal to testify, and the court gave jury instructions that included a reference to D's refusal to testify. The instructions also stated that such a refusal to testify could be taken by the jury as tending to indicate that inferences against D could be reasonably drawn. The Supreme Court granted certiorari.

**Issue.** Does a comment by the prosecutor and in the jury instructions relating to a defendant's refusal to testify deny the defendant due process?

**Held.** Yes. Judgment reversed.

♦ If this had been a federal trial, the comments would have been reversible error. Comment on the refusal to testify is a remnant of the inquisitorial system of criminal justice, which the Fifth Amendment prohibits.

♦ Although earlier federal cases invalidating such comments were based on a federal statute, the spirit of the self-incrimination privilege prohibits all such comments as a matter of basic due process. The Fifth Amendment privilege applies to the states as a matter of due process through the Fourteenth Amendment.

**Dissent** (Stewart, White, JJ.). D has not been compelled to be a witness against himself. Also, the court's instructions could benefit D by not leaving the jury with their own, untutored instincts to guide them in making inferences from D's silence.

**Comment.** Upon a defendant's request, the court may instruct the jury that the defendant has a constitutional right not to testify in his own defense and that no inference of guilt can be drawn therefrom. The Court has also held that such minimal instructions, even if given over a defendant's objections, do not violate the defendant's privilege. [*See* Lakeside v. Oregon, 435 U.S. 333 (1978)]

---

5. **Writings.** A writing can be as incriminating as testimony. However, the courts have recognized a difference between oral testimony and a pre-existing writing.

### 6. Order to Sign Documents--

## United States v. Doe, 465 U.S. 605 (1984).

**Facts.** During an investigation of corruption in the awarding of county and municipal contracts, a grand jury served subpoenas, demanding the production of business records, on the owner of several sole proprietorships (D). D filed a motion in federal district court to quash the subpoenas. The district court found that the act of producing the records would compel D to admit that the records existed, that they were in his possession, and that they were authentic. The court found that these communicative aspects warranted Fifth Amendment protection and granted D's motion except with respect to records required by law to be kept or disclosed to a public agency. The court of appeals affirmed, finding that the records were privileged. The court also rejected the government's attempt to compel delivery of the subpoenaed records because the government had not made a formal request for use immunity pursuant to 18 U.S.C. sections 6002 and 6003. The Supreme Court granted certiorari.

**Issue.** Does the Fifth Amendment privilege against compelled self-incrimination apply to the production of business records of a sole proprietorship?

**Held.** Yes. Judgment affirmed in part, reversed in part, and case remanded.

♦ In *Fisher v. United States*, 425 U.S. 391 (1976), this Court noted that the Fifth Amendment protects the person asserting the privilege only from compelled self-incrimination. Where the preparation of business records is voluntary, there is no compulsion. Thus, the contents of voluntarily prepared business records of a proprietor are not privileged.

♦ D does not claim that he prepared the records involuntarily or that the subpoenas would force him to restate, repeat, or affirm the truth of the records' contents. Therefore, the contents of the subpoenaed records in this case are not privileged.

♦ However, even if the records are not privileged, the act of production may be privileged if it has testimonial and incriminating aspects. Here, because the act of producing the records has testimonial aspects and an incriminating effect, the act of production is privileged and could not be compelled without a statutory grant of use immunity.

**Concurrence** (O'Connor, J.). The Fifth Amendment provides absolutely no protection for the contents of private papers of any kind.

**Concurrence and dissent** (Marshall, Brennan, JJ.). The majority's disagreement with the court of appeals' discussion of whether the Fifth Amendment protected the contents of the records did not call for reversal, because the court of appeals' judgment did not rest upon the disposition of this issue. I also disagree with Justice O'Connor's contention that the opinion in this case stands for the proposition that the Fifth Amendment provides absolutely no protection for the contents of private papers of any kind.

**Concurrence and dissent** (Stevens, J.). I dissent to the reversal of the judgment of the court of appeals. Its decision did not turn on whether the contents of the records were privileged, but on whether the act of producing them was privileged.

---

# XIII. FOUNDATIONAL EVIDENCE AND AUTHENTICATION

## A. INTRODUCTION

1. **Introduction.** Article IX of the Federal Rules of Evidence governs authentication and identification. The requirement of authentication or identification is a condition precedent to admissibility. The requirement is satisfied by evidence sufficient to support a finding that the matter in question is what its proponent claims. Some items may be self-authenticating, such as public documents, official publications, newspapers and periodicals, and acknowledged documents.

2. **Procedure.** The normal ways to authenticate and introduce evidence at a trial are: (i) have the exhibit marked for identification; (ii) have a witness testify about the exhibit to establish that it is what it purports to be; (iii) offer the exhibit into evidence; (iv) allow opposing counsel to examine the exhibit and object; (v) submit the exhibit to the court for examination; and (vi) seek a ruling from the court on admissibility.

## B. TANGIBLE OBJECTS

1. **Identifying Physical Evidence--**

## United States v. Johnson, 637 F.2d 1224 (9th Cir. 1980).

**Facts.** The United States prosecuted Johnson (D) for an assault that resulted in serious bodily injury. At trial, Papse, the victim, identified a long-handled ax, apparently with some hesitancy, as the weapon used to assault him. The ax had been found at D's residence and had no distinguishing marks. The district court admitted the ax over D's objection of insufficient authentication. D was convicted. D appeals.

**Issue.** Did the district court abuse its discretion in admitting the ax, identified only by the victim, into evidence?

**Held.** No. But conviction reversed and case remanded because of an error in a jury instruction.

♦ Although Papse's identification of the ax was not entirely free from doubt, he did say that he was "pretty sure" this was the weapon D had used against him, that he saw the ax in D's hand, and that he was personally familiar with this particular ax because he had used it in the past.

♦   From this testimony, a reasonable jury could have found that this ax was the weapon allegedly used in the assault, although it was not required to do so.

♦   Uncertainties in Papse's testimony went to its weight, not to admissibility of the ax.

**Comment.** Notice how little in the way of identification the court was willing to settle for. This partly reflects a general judicial attitude toward identification but also may be because this tangible evidence was not crucial to the case and therefore not worth any greater expenditure of effort. A weapon, like most tangible items, may be admitted in evidence even though not in precisely the same condition as at the time of the transaction or occurrence in which it figured, so long as the alteration is not material to the purpose for which it is offered.

---

## 2.   Chain of Custody--

## United States v. Howard-Arias, 679 F.2d 363 (4th Cir. 1982).

**Facts.** Howard-Arias (D) was a crew member on a fishing trawler called "Don Frank." The ship became disabled off the coast of Virginia. D and the other crew members were rescued by an Italian ship and turned over to the United States Coast Guard. A Coast Guard officer discovered bales of marijuana on the Don Frank. The Coast Guard attempted to tow the Don Frank into shore, but it sank. 240 bales of marijuana were salvaged, however. D was charged with drug-related violations. At trial, the government produced all but one of the agents involved in the chain of custody. D was convicted. He appeals, claiming the break in the chain of custody should have made the marijuana inadmissible.

**Issue.** If there is a break in the chain of custody for an item of evidence, must the evidence be excluded from trial?

**Held.** No. Judgment affirmed.

♦   The chain of custody rule is an aspect of authenticating evidence before it is admitted in court. The objective is to make sure the item is what it purports to be—in this case, marijuana seized from the Don Frank.

♦   When there is a break in the chain of custody, the ultimate question is whether the authentication testimony satisfied the court that it is improbable that the original item had been switched with another or otherwise tampered with. A break in the chain does not require that the evidence be excluded. The court must determine whether the break made the other authenticity evidence inadequate. The court uses its own discretion to resolve this question, and the court did not abuse that discretion in this case.

---

## C.  WRITINGS

1.  **General Rule.** As with all evidence, before any writing (or secondary evidence of its content) may be received in evidence, it must be authenticated; *i.e.,* the proponent must offer a foundation of evidence sufficient to support a finding that the document is genuine and what it purports to be. [Fed. R. Evid. 901; Cal. Evid. Code §1401]

    a.  **Not required if genuineness admitted.** Of course, this is not required if the genuineness of the document is admitted in the pleadings or by other evidence, or if the adverse party fails to raise timely objection to lack of foundation.

    b.  **Prima facie showing sufficient.** Authentication requires only enough evidence to establish a prima facie showing that the document is what it purports to be. If its genuineness is disputed, it is up to the jury to decide the question by a preponderance of the evidence.

2.  **Documents Requiring Independent Proof of Authenticity.** In most cases, the proponent of the writing must produce evidence apart from the document itself to show that it is genuine and is what it purports to be.

    a.  **Direct evidence of authenticity.**

        1)  **Testimony by subscribing witnesses.** At common law, this was the only method by which a deed, mortgage, or other private document could be authenticated; *i.e.,* a document would not be accepted as genuine unless it had been subscribed by attesting witnesses, who appeared in court to identify the document (unless such witnesses were unavailable). This is no longer required under modern law, although it is a valid way to authenticate a document. Probate law, not any evidentiary rules, may still require testimony of subscribing witnesses to authenticate wills.

        2)  **Testimony of other witnesses.** The testimony of any witness who saw the execution of the document, or heard the parties acknowledge the document, may be used to authenticate the document, whether he subscribed the document or not. [Fed. R. Evid. 901(b)(l); Cal. Evid. Code §1413]

        3)  **Opinion testimony as to handwriting identification.** A writing may also be authenticated by evidence of the genuineness of the

handwriting of the maker. Such evidence may be given by any person familiar with the handwriting of the supposed writer, or by expert testimony, or even by having the trier of fact compare it with some admittedly genuine document. [Fed. R. Evid. 901(b)(2)-(3); Cal. Evid. Code §1415 *et seq.*]

**b. Circumstantial evidence of authenticity.**

    **1) Admissions.** It may be shown that the party against whom the writing is offered has in the past either admitted its authenticity or acted upon it as if it were authentic.

    **2) Authentication by content.** A writing may also be authenticated by a showing that it contains information that is unlikely to have been known to anyone other than the person who is claimed to have written it, or is written in a manner unique to that person. [Fed. R. Evid. 901(b)(4); Cal. Evid. Code §1421]

        **a) Reply letter doctrine.** A writing may be authenticated by evidence that it was received in response to a communication sent to the author.

        **b) Connecting link.** When a series of correspondence between two persons is established, and a letter is shown to fit in as a connecting link between other letters in that series, that may be sufficient to authenticate the letter as being part of the series.

    **3) Authentication by content, location, address, and postmark--**

---

**United States v. Bagaric**, 706 F.2d 42 (2nd Cir. 1983).

---

**Facts.** Bagaric (D) and others, including Logarusic, were convicted of RICO violations. A letter discovered at Logarusic's house linked him with an unindicted co-racketeer, Miro Baresic. Logarusic appeals his conviction, claiming that the letter was not properly authenticated.

**Issue.** May a letter be authenticated by its contents, considered in light of where it was found and the postmark on the envelope?

**Held.** Yes. Judgment affirmed.

♦    The authentication requirement is satisfied by evidence sufficient to support a finding that the matter is what the proponent claims.

♦    The letter in this case was found at Logarusic's house. It was addressed to him and postmarked Asuncion, Paraguay, where Baresic lived. The letter was written to him and signed by Baresic. It also referred to the other defendants who lived in Chicago and referred to other people they both knew. This is sufficient evidence to authenticate the letter.

———

3.   **Self-Authenticating Documents.** Certain types of documents or records, such as notarized documents, certified copies of public records, etc., do not require independent proof of authenticity. Their nature is such that merely producing one of these documents establishes prima facie its own authentication. The burden then shifts to the adverse party to prove that the document is not what it purports to be or otherwise is not authentic.

## D.   TAPE RECORDINGS

1.   **Introduction.** Sound recordings can be problematic because they are susceptible to alterations. To use them as evidence, the prosecution must satisfy certain requirements designed to show that the recording is an accurate reproduction of relevant sounds previously audited by a witness.

2.   **Operator's Experience--**

———

**United States v. Biggins**, 551 F.2d 64 (5th Cir. 1977).

———

**Facts.** Lydes, who was a confidential informant for the Drug Enforcement Agency ("DEA"), arranged to buy drugs from Biggins (D). Several days later, Lydes and Wells, a DEA agent, met D, who agreed to sell them heroin later in the day at Lydes's apartment. Lydes's apartment was wired for surveillance. From across the street, Anderson, a DEA agent, monitored and recorded the conversation between D and Lydes in Lydes's apartment. During the conversation, D sold Wells the heroin. D was tried for drug offenses. The prosecution used the original tape of the conversation in Lydes's apartment, together with a re-recorded filtered version. D was convicted. D appeals.

**Issue.** Should the sound recordings have been admitted into evidence at D's trial?

**Held.** Yes. Judgment affirmed.

♦   The dangers presented by tape recordings used as evidence require a court to pay special attention to authentication issues. The judge has discretion to determine whether a recording may be used. Generally, the prosecution must show that: (i) the recording device was capable of recording the conversation; (ii) the operator was competent; (iii) the recording is authentic and correct, without changes; (iv) the speakers are identified; and (v) the conversation was not induced.

- In this case, the prosecution did not establish that Anderson was trained or competent. However, Anderson did show that he was familiar with the techniques of electronic surveillance, and it would be reasonable to infer that he was competent to use the equipment.

- Anderson did not know who re-recorded and filtered the original tape of the conversation, and there was no evidence about the competence of this person. This would be a problem if the prosecution had not also used the original recording or if there was no other evidence that the re-recording was accurate.

- Although Anderson testified that the re-recording was a duplicate of the original tape, he did nothing to verify that the original was a faithful recording of the original conversation in the first place. For example, he did not replay the tape with the informant to have him verify the accuracy of the recording. This would be a fatal defect if there were no other evidence to authenticate the tape. Here, Lydes and Wells testified about the conversation, and this testimony verified the content of the tape recording.

---

## E. TELEPHONE CONVERSATIONS

1. **Introduction.** Telephone conversations that are not recorded can be difficult to authenticate, unless the witness has some clear basis for recognizing the caller's voice.

2. **Single Phone Call--**

---

### United States v. Pool, 660 F.2d 547 (5th Cir. 1981).

---

**Facts.** Pool (D) and other defendants, including Loye, were charged and convicted of importing $60 million worth of marijuana into the United States. Loye's involvement was established through evidence that he had called a DEA agent. The agent testified at trial that he received a phone call from a person who identified himself as "Chip." Because Loye had used this nickname during the investigation, the agent identified Loye as the caller. However, the agent had never previously spoken with Loye, he did not record the conversation, and he never made any voice comparison with Loye. D appeals from his conviction.

**Issue.** Is a phone call properly authenticated if the only evidence of the identity of the caller is the caller's self-identification?

**Held.** No. Judgment reversed.

- The standard of admissibility of voice identification testimony is prima facie, and circumstantial evidence may be used to meet this standard. However, prior cases have established that a telephone call "out of the blue" from one who identifies himself as X may not be, in itself, sufficient authentication that the call is in fact coming from X.

♦ In this case, there is insufficient evidence to support the conclusion that the DEA agent actually heard Loye's voice. The caller's use of the nickname "Chip" does not constitute a prima facie case that Loye was the caller. There is too great a possibility that someone else used Loye's nickname.

---

## F. REAL OR DEMONSTRATIVE EVIDENCE

1. **Introduction.** Real or demonstrative evidence is evidence that can be directly presented to the fact finder (*e.g.*, a gun or a knife). The testimony of witnesses regarding such evidence is not required; the evidence speaks for itself.

2. **Types of Real Evidence.**

   a. **Original evidence.** Real evidence may be the original thing itself, *i.e.*, real evidence that has some connection with an issue in the case (*e.g.*, the murder weapon in a homicide case). When the thing cannot be brought into court, the trial judge may permit the jury to go to view the object. For example, the jury may see the scene of the crime. The majority view is that such views may be considered as evidence.

   b. **Prepared evidence.** Real evidence may be prepared for demonstration. For example, tape recordings, sketches, models, photographs, maps, courtroom experiments, etc., may be presented.

   c. **Direct evidence.** Real evidence may be offered to prove some fact about the object itself. For example, if the issue is whether P was injured, his mangled arm might be shown to the jury.

   d. **Circumstantial evidence.** Real evidence may also be presented to raise an inference as to the existence or nonexistence of some fact that is in issue.

3. **Problems of Admissibility.**

   a. **Relevancy.** All real evidence must pass the basic relevancy test in order to be admitted in evidence. In addition, real evidence may be excluded if it is too prejudicial. For example, a court might hold it too prejudicial when P offers to show his half-severed leg.

**b. Authentication.** All real evidence must be identified and its connection with the case explained. Witnesses are called to do this. Such authentication has two purposes:

1) The objects presented as evidence must be shown to be the ones that are being testified about. For example, a purported photograph of the scene of the crime must be an actual and close representation of the real scene to be admitted.

2) The possibility of tampering with the evidence must be excluded. For example, it must be shown that a tape recording has not been altered or a photograph "touched up." This is done by showing the "chain of custody."

**c. Discretion.** In making these rulings the trial judge is given wide discretion.

# XIV. THE BEST EVIDENCE DOCTRINE

## A. INTRODUCTION

1.  **Introduction.** The "best evidence" rule would he better named the "original writing" rule. It does not require that the best or most probative evidence available be produced, merely that an original writing be produced to prove the contents thereof, unless it is unavailable. [Fed. R. Evid. 1002]

2.  **Rationale.** The rule is intended to prevent fraud or mistakes that could result from allowing oral testimony or copies instead of the original. Slight difference in written words or symbols may make a vast difference in meaning. For the same reason, witnesses may usually not speculate about the meaning or content of documents.

## B. DEFINING A WRITING, RECORDING, OR PHOTOGRAPH

1.  **Basic Rule.** The Federal Rules of Evidence provide specific definitions of the types of evidence subject to the best evidence rule. The rule applies to more than merely written documents.

    a.  **Writings and recordings.** "Writings" and "recordings" consist of letters, words, or numbers, or their equivalent, set down by handwriting, typewriting, printing, photostating, photographing, magnetic impulse, mechanical or electronic recording, or other form of data compilation.

    b.  **Photographs.** "Photographs" include still photographs, X-ray films, videotapes, and motion pictures.

    c.  **Original.** An "original" of a writing or recording is the writing or recording itself or any counterpart intended to have the same effect by a person executing or issuing it. An "original" of a photograph includes the negative or any print therefrom. If data are stored in a computer or similar device, any printout or other output readable by sight, shown to reflect the data accurately, is an "original."

    d.  **Duplicate.** A "duplicate" is a counterpart produced by the same impression as the original, or from the same matrix, or by means of photography, including enlargements and miniatures, or by mechanical or electronic rerecording, or by chemical reproduction, or by other equivalent techniques which accurately reproduce the original.

## 2. Not Applicable to Chattels--

---

## United States v. Duffy, 454 F.2d 809 (5th Cir. 1972).

---

**Facts.** At Duffy's (D's) trial for transporting a stolen vehicle in interstate commerce, he contended that he got to California by hitchhiking, not by transporting the stolen car there. To connect D with the car, the prosecution established that D worked in the body shop where the car had been sent for repairs and that D and the car disappeared over the same weekend. The prosecution also presented testimony, including that of a police officer and an F.B.I. agent, who testified that they had found two suitcases in the car's trunk and, in one of them, a white shirt bearing the laundry mark "D-U-F." D objected, contending that, since the shirt bore an inscription, it must be produced as the best evidence. The objection was overruled. D was convicted. D appeals.

**Issue.** Did the trial court's refusal to require the shirt itself instead of allowing testimony describing the shirt and laundry mark violate the best evidence rule?

**Held.** No. Judgment affirmed.

♦ Although the phrase "best evidence rule" is frequently used in general terms, the rule itself is applicable only to the proof of the contents of a writing. It does not apply to chattels, *i.e.*, to tangibles.

♦ The shirt with a laundry mark would not, under ordinary understanding, be considered a writing.

♦ When the disputed evidence, such as the shirt in this case, is an object bearing a mark or inscription, and is, therefore, a chattel and a writing, the trial judge has discretion to treat the evidence as a chattel or as a writing.

♦ The trial judge did not abuse his discretion. Because the writing involved in this case was simple, there was little danger that the witness would inaccurately remember the terms of the "writing." Also, the terms of the "writing" were by no means central or critical to the case against D.

**Comment.** Where an inscription is complex or detailed, where fair evaluation requires precise information about the exact inscription, and where the inscribed chattel can be produced without unreasonable expense, hardship, or delay, a court might well require the chattel in preference to testimony about its inscription.

---

## C. APPLICATION OF RULE

### 1. Original Writing.

a. **Meaning.** The best evidence rule applies to all printed or written documents. It includes photographs, recordings, and other forms of data. [Fed. R. Evid. 1001]

b. **Duplicate originals.** Carbon copies, photocopies, microfilms, etc., are duplicates. A duplicate may be admissible as the original unless:

   1) The authenticity of the original is genuinely disputed; or

   2) Admission of the duplicate would be unfair (*e.g.*, only part of the original was reproduced).

2. **Limitations.** The rule is limited in application to specified situations.

   a. **Official records.** The best evidence rule applies only to private writings. Properly authenticated copies of official documents or recorded writings may be used instead of the originals. [Fed. R. Evid. 1005]

   b. **Collateral contents.** The rule applies when secondary evidence is offered to prove the contents of the original writing, but not when the writing itself is not closely related to the controlling issues. [Fed. R. Evid. 1004(d)] In other words, if the existence of the document, but not its contents, is significant, the rule would not apply.

   c. **Limited to cases where writing contents in issue--**

---

**Meyers v. United States**, 171 F.2d 800 (D.C. Cir. 1948), cert. denied, 336 U.S. 912 (1949).

---

**Facts.** Meyers (D) was indicted for suborning perjury, and Lamarre was indicted for perjury, based on Lamarre's testimony before a Senate subcommittee. At D's trial, the government attorney who had examined Lamarre before the subcommittee testified as to what Lamarre had said under oath. Later in the trial, the transcripts of the subcommittee proceedings were admitted. D was convicted and appeals.

**Issue.** Does the best evidence rule preclude oral testimony about what was said at an earlier proceeding when written transcripts of the proceeding are available?

**Held.** No. Judgment affirmed.

♦ The federal courts have limited the application of the best evidence rule to cases where the contents of the writing are to be proved. Here, the issue was what Lamarre had said, not what the transcript contained. Perjury may be proved by the oral testimony of anyone who heard it, as well as by the reporter who recorded the perjurious statements.

◆　The best evidence rule applies only to documentary evidence. When a contested factual issue may be proved by reference to a writing, such as a transcript, other forms of proof are not excluded. Only when the content of the writing is disputed does the rule apply.

**Dissent.** The principle of using the best evidence precludes allowing oral testimony when a written transcript is available. Furthermore, in this case, the transcript was not even given to D until during the trial. Also, when the government attorney testified as to what Lamarre had said before the subcommittee, the attorney admitted that he did not remember Lamarre's exact testimony.

---

d.　**Admissions.** If a party admits the contents, the admission may be used without explaining the non-production of the original writing. [Fed. R. Evid. 1007]

## D.　PRODUCTION OF ORIGINAL EXCUSED

1.　**Reasons for Not Producing the Original**. An original writing may be "unavailable" for several reasons. The trial judge determines whether the reason for nonproduction justifies use of secondary evidence. [Fed. R. Evid. 1008]

a.　**Lost or destroyed.** The best evidence rule does not apply when the original writing has been lost or destroyed without fault of the proponent of the secondary evidence. [Fed. R. Evid. 1004(1)] Most states limit the type of secondary evidence that may be used to prove the contents of lost wills, however.

b.　**Unobtainable.** When the original writing is in the possession of a third person who is outside the court's subpoena power (outside the state), the rule usually does not apply. [Fed. R. Evid. 1004(2)]

c.　**Voluminous writings**. If the original writings are so voluminous that it would be impractical to produce them in court, secondary evidence, *e.g.*, a summary, may be introduced as long as the originals are available for inspection by the adverse party. [Fed. R. Evid. 1006]

d.　**Opponent's possession.** If the adverse party controls or possesses the original writing and fails to produce it on reasonable advance notice, secondary evidence may be admitted. [Fed. R. Evid. 1004(3)]

2.　**Reasonable Search Required--**

---

**Sylvania Electric Products v. Flanagan,** 352 F.2d 1005 (1st Cir. 1965).

---

**Facts.** Sylvania Electric Products (D) contracted with a general contractor to build a parking lot. The general contractor was not required to haul off material that was removed to build the parking lot, so D agreed with Flanagan (P) to have P haul the material. This was an oral agreement. D was to pay P $13 per hour per truck. P used 1,932 ½ truck hours and billed D over $25,000. When D refused to pay, P sued for breach of contract. At trial, P offered into evidence copies of bills and a tally sheet that summarized the number of trucks on the job and the hours they worked. The jury found for P. D appeals.

**Issue.** May secondary evidence be used where the proponent has not made a reasonable search for the original records?

**Held.** No. Judgment vacated and case remanded.

♦     D claims that the best evidence rule should have prevented the court from admitting the summary tally sheet. The best evidence rule requires that the best available evidence must be used to prove disputed facts. The best evidence of P's claim is the truck hour records, which are on the individual tally sheets. Instead of producing these, however, P simply prepared summary sheets. The summary is thus secondary evidence of the content of the originals.

♦     During the trial, P said that he had the original tally sheets that were used to make the summarized tally sheet, but he never produced them. There was insufficient evidence that the originals were unavailable or that P had made a reasonable search for them. He merely said that he would search for them, but there is no evidence about the extent of the search he made, or even if he actually did search.

♦     Where the missing original writings are in dispute and are the foundation of the claim, the proponent of the evidence must show that he made all reasonable efforts to obtain the originals. P failed to do so in this case. The court failed to make findings that the originals were unavailable and should not have admitted the secondary evidence.

---

# TABLE OF CASES
(Page numbers of briefed cases in bold)

# NOTES

# NOTES

# NOTES

# NOTES

# NOTES

**NOTES**